Perfect Da...

CRETE

Travel with **Insider Tips**

Contents

 TOP 10   4

That Crete Feeling   6

For chapters: See inside front cover

to be missed!
TOP 10 hits – from the absolute No. 1 to No. 10 –
⊳ you plan your tour of the most important sights.

KNOSSOS ➤ 80

⎯e reconstructed palace of
⎯⎯ossos (photo left), near the
⎯⎯and's capital of Iraklio, gives
⎯⎯itors an idea of the splendour
⎯⎯ the more than 3,500-year-old
⎯noan culture.

ARCHAIOLOGIKO MOUSEIO, IRAKLIO ➤ 54

⎯e museum's rich collection
⎯ art, ritual objects and every-
⎯ay utensils, unearthed by
⎯chaeologists in Crete, are
⎯l beautifully exhibited and
⎯learly explained.

CHANIA ➤ 138

⎯ver 500 years of Venetian rule left
⎯heir mark on Crete, and nowhere
⎯s this more evident than in Chania,
Crete's second largest city.

4 RETHIMNON ➤ 142

A particularly large number of
Ottoman-era minarets soar above
the city; and its harbour is the most
picturesque in Crete.

FARANGI SAMARIAS ➤ 146

A hike through the Samaria
Gorge, in the White Mountains,
is an exciting adventure that
combines physical challenge with
great nature, and it finishes off
with a ferry trip.

6 GORTIS ➤ 87

Many of the ruins of the former
Roman capital are picturesquely
scattered through an ancient olive
grove.

7 PHAISTOS (FESTOS) ➤ 90

The Minoan palace of Phaistos
lies in a scenic location on a hill
overlooking a fertile plain between
Mount Ida and the Asterousia
Mountains.

8 GOURNIA ➤ 110

The excavation of this small
Minoan country town gives one
a vivid impression of how the
island's ordinary people lived more
than 3,500 years ago.

9 MONI ARKADIOU ➤ 148

In a solitary location on a high
plateau, this Renaissance monastery is a national shrine and
symbol of Crete's struggle for
independence – hundreds of
Cretans sacrificed their life
here during a rebellion against
Turkish rule.

10 AGIOS NIKOLAOS ➤ 112

The small, picturesque town in the
east boasts a freshwater lake as
a fishing port, an excellent museum
and a former leper colony as an
excursion destination.

THAT
CRETE

Find out what makes the island tick, experience its unique flair – just like the Cretans themselves.

TAKE A *VOLTÁ* AT SUNDOWN

After they finish work, and before they have their late dinner, Cretans love to stroll up and down in front of the cafés and tavernas – to see and be seen – and to stop for a glass of ouzo or *rakí*. Ideal places for a stroll include **Chania's** harbour (► 138), the main street in **Paleochora** (► 156), which is closed to traffic in the evening, and the lakeside promenade at **Agios Nikolaos** (► 112).

LYRA AND *LAOUTO*

The traditional music that delights Cretans young and old is played on the *lyra* and *laouto*. The melodies express tales of love and suffering, longing for liberty and the struggle for freedom. The verses are often spontaneously changed to make references to those present. The *lyra* and *laouto* are an essential part of any Cretan wedding; they are sometimes played on the spur of the moment in small *kafeníon* and can be heard regularly in many taverns in the old sections of Rethimnon and Chania.

AN EVENING WITH FRIENDS

Cretans do not like to eat alone or to have a cosy tête-à-tête, a meal is considered a social occasion so they prefer to get together with friends and acquaintances. And, they do not just order for themselves. It is more common to have the waiter bring an assortment of dishes that are then placed in the middle of the table and everyone helps themselves. Too much food is often ordered, as there must always be some leftovers. Empty plates mean that the diners were not being generous and that some may not have had enough to eat. Perfect for Cretan dinners of this kind are the *ouzerís* and *rakadiko* on Odos Vernardou in Rethimnon (► 142), Odos Marinelli in Iraklio (► 49) and in the harbour at Chania (► 138).

HEAD FOR THE MOUNTAINS

When they want to enjoy a short holiday, Cretans usually head up to the mountains, except at the height of summer. Many of the mountain villages offer them – and tourists from abroad – traditionally furnished guest houses, hotels with a lot of local colour and some excellent cuisine. It is always easy to strike up a conversation with the locals in one of the village coffee houses, the air is pure and clear, and the donkeys, dogs and roosters make sure there is also a gentle nocturnal chorus.

FEELING

Chania's Venetian harbour is ideal for a promenade stroll

That Crete Feeling

The **Lasithiou Plateau** (➤ 168) and the large village of **Anogia** on the Psiloritis (➤ 96) are ideal destinations this kind of brief getaway.

CHILLING TO GOOD MUSIC

The modern pavement cafés on Odos Chandakos and Odos Korai in **Iraklio** (➤ 49) are always packed with young people from early in the morning until late at night. These places make you feel as though you are in one gigantic open-air club; you can spend hours in a single café and have any number of great conversations.

COUNTLESS SEASIDE PLEASURES

Crete's coastline is 1,046km (650mi) long with a variety of beautiful beaches There are lagoon beaches, such as in **Elafonisi** and **Balos** (⊞ 188 A4) where you will feel like you are in a tropical paradise, and beaches lined with palm groves such as in **Vaï** and **Preveli**. Some of the beaches are more than 10km (6mi) long as in **Georgioupolis** and **Rethimnon**, and in other places you will discover tiny, secluded bays such as the Red Beach near **Matala**. Some of them slope gently into the water, making them ideal for young children, while others drop off steeply enough for swimming as in **Sougia** (⊞ 188 C2) and **Kato Zakros**.

IMPRESSIVE GORGES AND RAVINES

The world-famous Samaria Gorge might be the longest but it is by no means the only scenic gorge on the island of Crete. More than 100 gorges and ravines, with differing levels of accessibility, lie waiting for the adventurous. The locals explore them with mountaineering clubs while specialist travel agencies offer guided tours for tourists (www.vamossa.gr; www.ansovillas.com; www.happy-walker.com). And, the really daring can even bungee jump 136m (446ft) into the **Aradena Gorge** (⊞ 189 D2 ➤ 48) near Chora Sfakion.

DISCOVER IDYLLIC ISLANDS

There are several small islands just off the coast of Crete where you can spend a day soaking up the laid-back island life. In summer, small excursion boats take people out to them so that they can go swimming: from Limenas Chersonisou to **Dia** (⊞ 192 B5), from Rethimnon to **Marathi** (⊞ 189 E4) in Souda Bay, from Chania to **Agii Theodori** (⊞ 188 C4), from Kissamos to **Gramvousa** (⊞ 188 A5), from Ierapetra to **Chrisi** (➤ 124) and from Paleochora to **Gavdos** (➤ 154). All you need to take with you is your sunblock.

Mountain biking in the Therisiano Gorge

The Magazine

The Magazine

FIRST A CRETAN,
THEN A GREEK

**Nikos Kazantzakis, Crete's beloved author of *Zorba the Greek*
(1946), declared he was "first a Cretan, then a Greek",
and this is a belief still shared by Cretans of all ages, from
all walks of life, and from all corners of the island.**

Cretans spent decades striving for *enosis* (union) with Greece, achieved in
1913, yet it was motivated not by a desire to reconnect with their roots,
but by a need to protect their land. Security concerns stemmed from the
Battle of Crete and a long history of invasions. Physically separated
from the rest of the country by the Sea of Crete, Greece's largest island
has always been vulnerable.

Crete's centuries of resistance to foreign occupation (▶ 20) and its
tireless struggle for freedom have left a deep imprint on the soul. Cretans
are survivors who fiercely value their independence and self-reliance.
During local festivals and celebrations old men wear costumes with a dagger
or firearm tucked into their waist sash, symbolising their readiness to
resist and the value of freedom and *philotimo* (honour) in Cretan tradition.

Symbol of Mourning

You'll notice old women wearing black. Traditionally, Cretans wore black for up to three years out of respect for a dead relative. Foreign oppression brought such loss and mourning that it virtually became the national colour.

Elefthérios Venizélos

Crete's revered statesman Elefthérios Venizélos (1864–1936) was one man who didn't hesitate to resist. Born in Mournies village near Chania, he fought against Turkish rule and in 1897 led a protest that saw the first raising of the Greek flag on Crete. Venizélos became prime minister of Greece in 1910 and under his rule *enosis* was achieved. Streets and squares throughout Greece bear his name.

All In The Family

To understand the Cretan character, look to the bedrock of island life – the land and the family. Family means extended family and it's not uncommon for several generations to live together under one roof and for family members to help each other in times of need.

Socially, different generations mix happily in and outside of the home. Don't be surprised to see youths in the latest fashions and hip haircuts sitting beside moustachioed grandfathers in baggy breeches and high boots at a local bar. Though young people are increasingly leaving rural areas to study or work in cities, most return to the village for Easter, family celebrations, festivals and harvests.

Two generations on one motorcycle in Rethimnon

The Magazine

Cretans branded as liars

Some 2,500 years ago, Cretan philosopher Epimenides said all Cretans were liars, St Paul quoted him, and it stuck. Most likely the claim stems from an ancient Cretan belief in a fertility god who died and was reborn annually. The Cretan "Zeus" was buried beneath Mount Giouchtas near Knossos, but the northern Greeks, for whom their Zeus was immortal, were outraged by this heresy and branded them liars.

What is true is that Cretans enjoy a good story. They love to talk and can be prone to exaggeration and making promises that might be forgotten the next day. It's all part of their mercurial nature – alternately warm and indifferent, relaxed and passionate, but always genuine.

A Stranger and a Guest

The Greek word *xenoi* has a dual meaning: "stranger" and "guest". It is the custom that a stranger is automatically a guest in one's country and in one's home. Although the high tourist numbers threaten this tradition, expect to experience sudden gestures of hospitality – fresh figs from someone's tree, a complimentary *rakí*, an invitation to share a meal. Such generosity doesn't need to be repaid, for Cretans take pleasure in giving. Show your appreciation with a smile and a simple *efharisto* (thanks in Greek).

Cretan Institutions

The *kafeníon* (café), a coffeehouse-cum-bar, is to Crete what the pub is to Britain. There's at least one in every village or town and you'll recognise it by the men sitting outside drinking strong Greek coffee or brandy, playing cards or backgammon, exchanging news, and arguing politics.

Fishing boats in Iraklio harbour

Oranges grow prolifically all over the island

The *kafeníon* is a male domain, as much an unofficial men's club as a public café, and although few Cretan women buck tradition by joining the men, exceptions are made for visitors. These days, local women, along with the younger generation, prefer to drink their Nescafé *frappés* in the many stylish contemporary cafés that line the waterfronts and squares of Cretan cities and towns.

You'll also notice that chairs generally face outwards to the street rather face each other. Cretans enjoy people-watching and love nothing more than to watch the *voltá*, or evening stroll. Introduced by the Venetians, the *voltá* is a time for socialising and a chance to dress up and see and be seen. Whether around the town square or along a seafront promenade, families and couples stroll arm in arm, stopping to chat with friends, while groups of young people gossip and flirt.

Spend some time in one place and you'll quickly appreciate Crete's strong café culture and the rituals and cycles of business at different cafés throughout the day – one crowded with old ladies in the morning might be closed by the afternoon, while another that looks shut down will be buzzing with students by night.

The *kafeníon* are full of men playing backgammon

THE RITUAL-LOVING MINOANS

The ancient Minoans, were an aesthetic, creative, ritual-loving people, if we can believe the pretty scenes depicted on pottery, frescoes and mosaics at Crete's museums and archaeological sites.

Crete was home to the Minoans, Europe's first civilisation, from around 3000BC when their culture flourished, until 1100BC. Amazingly, evidence of its greatness lay hidden until the 20th century when Englishman Arthur Evans excavated Knossos (▶ 80). Evans named the Minoans after the mythical Greek King Minos. It turned out that "Minos" was not a name but a title, like Egypt's pharaoh or Rome's caesar, and many more rulers bore this name.

These priest-kings built extravagant palaces at Knossos, Phaistos, Malia and Zakros, where they presided over a rich artistic culture that was obsessed with rituals.

The Art of Life

Most of what we know about the Minoans has been gleaned from their beautiful artworks. Vivid frescoes once decorated the walls of palaces, depicting scenes from Minoan life. These vibrant, paintings, made colourful from plants, minerals and shellfish, were skilfully executed, incorporating dynamic movement and sensuality. Women's skin was painted white and men's red, suggesting women may have played a powerful role in society or spent their days as ladies of leisure while the men worked outside toiling the fields.

THE SNAKE GODDESS

A potent Minoan religious figure that you'll see in figurines in museums and shops was that of the Snake Goddess, a woman holding a snake in each hand. Her bare breasts symbolised fertility while the snake, which sheds its skin, symbolised healing and rebirth (picture ➤ 56).

Exquisite sculptures, pottery, mosaics and decorative arts suggest that the Minoans lived an ancient version of the "good life". Their palace homes had roof terraces, light wells, baths and sophisticated plumbing systems. They were well fed, with huge granaries and giant vessels called *pithoi* which stored wine and olive oil. They were also great seafarers, trading their agricultural produce far and wide to acquire copper and tin to produce bronze, and gold, silver and precious stones to create jewellery and works of art.

One of the most curious facts about the Minoan's palaces is that they were built without fortifications, suggesting they lived peacefully and didn't fear attacks from enemies.

Dances with Bulls

Greece may be the birthplace of the Olympic games, but long before the first torch was carried through a stadium the Minoans were apparently turning somersaults over the horns of charging bulls. The Minoans loved games and athletic contests and bull-leaping satisfied both their appetite for sport and religious obligation. Images on artworks (picture ➤ 16)

The Magazine

THE MINOAN AGES

Archaeologists break down the Minoan civilisation into four main periods:

- **Pre-Palace period** (2600–1900BC). Bronze Age culture develops on Crete.
- **Old Palace period** (1900–1700BC). First Minoan palaces built but destroyed by earthquakes.
- **New Palace period** (1700–1450BC). Grand new palaces built and the civilisation reaches its height.
- **Post-Palace period** (1450–1100BC). Minoan civilisation declines and Mycenaeans move in.

suggest that Minoan athletes would grab a charging bull by the horns, somersault over its back, and land on their feet with arms raised in victory, and that both men and women took part in these dramatic feats, requiring great courage, agility and skill.

Spanish bullfighters claim bull-leaping is impossible, leading some scholars to suggest the scenes may only be symbolic. Representing virility, bulls had great significance in Minoan society. They were shaped into figurines and painted on vases, enormous sculpted "horns of consecration" adorned palace walls, and ceremonial drinking vessels called *rhytons* were carved into the shape of a bull's head.

In sacrificial rites related to agricultural cycles, a bull was captured and bound, its throat cut and its blood drained into the sacred cups. The ritual was thought to honour the bull and connect Minoans to their divine life force. Whether or not it actually occurred, bull-leaping may have symbolised the triumph of man over the forces of nature.

Somersaults over the horns of a bull – religious ritual or purely symbolic?

Prince of the Lilies fresco from Knossos   A Knossos fresco depicting a procession

Disastrous Ending

However, the Minoans weren't to triumph and their civilisation came to a sudden end around 1450BC, when a catastrophe occurred that destroyed all of their palaces. Many believe the volcanic eruption on nearby Santorini (Thira) created a deluge of tidal waves, earthquakes and fires on Crete, which could explain the charred remains found at palaces. Other scholars favour theories of invaders, such as the Mycenaeans, or a rebellion against the palace rulers. Whatever the cause, within 200 years the Minoans had all but disappeared; the reason remains a mystery.

MYTH OF THE MINOTAUR

Legend has it that Poseidon, god of the sea, sent King Minos a white bull, but when he later requested it be sacrificed Minos couldn't bring himself to kill the beautiful animal. In revenge the angry god caused the king's wife, Pasiphae, to fall in love with the bull and their mating produced the Minotaur, a creature with a bull's head and man's body. Minos kept the monster in a labyrinth beneath the palace and every nine years 14 youths were shipped from Athens and fed to the Minotaur. When Theseus, son of Athens' king, heard of this he vowed to stop the slaughter. Volunteering to be one of the victims, he entered the palace, seduced Minos's daughter Ariadne, who gave him a sword and ball of thread with which to kill the bull, and miraculously found his way out of the labyrinth.

The *BEAT*
of Crete

Watch a performance of live music in a restaurant or bar and witness how the locals are moved to tears and passionately join in for the chorus, and you'll appreciate how deeply music is embedded in the Cretan soul.

The *Mantinada*, *Rizitika* and *Erotokriti*

Dating back to the 5th century BC, the *Mantinada* is made up of rhyming couplets containing 15 syllables. The songs typically express every kind of emotion, especially the extremes of joy and sadness related to love.

Another popular musical form is *Rizitika* or rebel music. Originating in the White Mountains in the Chania province, the songs are mostly performed at weddings, baptisms and celebrations.

Participants need to be fit to perform the lively Cretan dances

Erotokriti are folk songs derived from the 10,000-line *Erotokritos* (tried
y love) epic written by Vitsentzos Kornáros (► 119) in the 16th century.
ingers in Crete often perform songs based on parts of the *Erotokritos*,
lthough some have been known to perform the whole poem in concert!

The Instruments of Music

The key instruments of Cretan music
that you'll see used are the *lyra* and
laouto. The *lyra* is a three-stringed,
pear-shaped instrument, traditionally
made of mulberry wood and played
on the knee like an upright violin.
It's normally accompanied by the
laouto, a type of lute that has four
pairs of strings. These days the
laouto (photo left) is popular as a
solo instrument as well.

The *lyra* player will often sing as
well and will alternate between
singing passages and soloing on
the instrument, while the *laouto*
accompanies. The traditional music
s a unique mix, sometimes sounding like an Irish jig and at other times
ike sounds reminiscent of the Middle East.

Where to See Live Music

Live music performed on these revered instruments is still immensely popular,
especially in Rethimnon (Odos Vernardou) and Chania (Odos Kondilaki).
Look for tavernas that have images of musical instruments on their signs
outside and you're pretty much assured that at some stage of the night –
whether it's planned or spontaneous (often there are instruments hanging
on the walls!) there will be a performance.

Insider Tip

On a good night, a performance can last for hours with much improvis-
ing and trading of complex musical motifs between the musicians. The
intoxicating mix of the music coupled with the effects of a few shots of *rakí*
makes for a memorable night out!

Musical Masters

The music shops of Iraklio are a good source of authentic Cretan music.
Look out for Nikos Xilouris (one of the greatest players), and his brother
Antonis, known as Psarantonis. Thanassis Skordalos is another contender
for the title of "the greatest".

Insider Tip

Foreign Influences
& EXOTIC FLAVOURS

Crete's unique social character and exotic flavour is the result of centuries of foreign influence, from the demise of the Minoans until the early 20th century. Successive occupations have shaped the architectural landscape, complex cuisine, heartfelt music, and strength of character of the Cretan people.

When you're sitting in a café in Crete, people-watching, watch the Cretans at the next table for a while. You'd be forgiven for mistaking them for Italians with their stylish dress, confident demeanour, and hand gesturing, and their musical Cretan dialect even sounds more Italian than Greek. Watch a traditional three-piece band perform in a taverna and you'll detect Turkish and Arab influences in the music. And in the cuisine – the Cretan *mezedes* are very similar to those served up in Turkey and the Middle East.

The Greeks

Mycenaean warriors from the Peloponnese were the first to invade Crete. They ruled Crete until their civilisation fell into decline shortly after the Trojan War. As their power waned, the northern Greek Dorians

Minaret of Nerantzes Mosque, Rethimnon

moved in to establish city-states, which you can see at Gortis, Lato and elsewhere. The original Cretans retreated to the mountains, which is why these days villagers from the interior make claims to be the purest Cretans.

The Romans

Conquering Crete in 67BC, the Romans established their capital at Gortis (►87) and built aqueducts, irrigation systems, roads, odeons, theatres, and pretty arched stone bridges, one of which you can see

TIMELINE

1450–1100BC Mycenaean period
1100–67BC Dorian period
67BC–AD337 Roman rule
337–824 First Byzantine period
824–961 Arab occupation
961–1204 Second Byzantine period
1204–1669 Venetian period
1669–1898 Ottoman period
1898 Crete gains autonomy
1913 *Enosis* (union) with Greece
1941–45 German occupation during World War II

Left: Koules fortress, Iraklio

The Magazine

at Vrisses, 32km (20mi) from Chania. St Paul brought Christianity to Crete in AD59.

The Byzantines

With the fall of the Western Roman Empire, Crete became part of the Byzantine Empire, ruled from Constantinople. During the first and second Byzantine periods, Christianity and art flourished and splendid monasteries and churches were built, many still standing today, such as the exquisite Arkadi (➤ 148) and Preveli (➤ 152) monasteries and several churches elsewhere on the island.

WHAT'S IN A NAME?

Crete's capital Iraklio has been known by many names. A port under the Romans, called Herakleium, after the Arab conquest it was fortified and named Rabdh-el-Khandak (Castle of the Moat) or Chandax. In medieval times the Venetians called the city and island Candia, while under Ottoman rule, it was Megalo Kastro (Great fortress). Iraklio (Iraklion, Heraklion) was adopted in 1922.

The Arabs

The Saracens, a band of Arabs who had been expelled from Spain and Alexandria, captured Crete in the 9th century. Gortis and other cities were destroyed, and Chandax (Iraklio) became a pirate den and slave market. The Byzantine general Nikephoros Phokas retook the island in 961 after a grisly siege in which captured Saracens were decapitated and their heads catapulted over the fortress walls. Little remains of this dark period.

Dionysius and Ariadne mosaic in Chania's Archaeological Museum

The Veli Pasha Mosque in Rethimnon, the oldest mosque in the city, is a legacy of Ottoman rule

The Venetians

Following the breakup of the Byzantine Empire, Crete was sold to Venice for 1,000 pieces of silver. Venetian rule, which lasted 465 years, brought prosperity, culture and the great fortresses, harbours, mansions, buildings, and fountains which you can see in Rethimnon, Chania and Iraklio.

The Ottomans

The Ottomans first attacked Chania in 1645, but it was another 24 years before they occupied Crete. Under Ottoman rule the island fell into economic and artistic decline and Christians were persecuted. The Cretans continuously rebelled, launching attacks from mountain strongholds. Splendid stone mosques with pretty minarets, and wooden Ottoman buildings boasting hanging balconies remain from this period, in Rethimnon and Chania.

WRITERS & ARTISTS

The Greeks invented literature with the *Odyssey* and the *Iliad* and created some of the world's most exquisite Byzantine painting, but the Cretans can be thanked for producing three of the world's most celebrated artists, the influential painter El Greco, the much-admired author Nikos Kazantzakis, and the Nobel Prize-winning poet Odysseus Elytis.

Odysseus Elytis, the Poet

The Cretan poet Odysseus Elytis (1911–96) was born in Iraklio to a wealthy family from the island of Lesbos, a source of inspiration to Elytis. His poetry was musical in form and rich in imagery inspired by myths and legends. While his earlier poems celebrated nature and the senses, his later, darker, work focused on suffering and grieving. Becoming a popular war poet, Elytis wrote potently about his experiences fighting the Germans during World War II. He was awarded the Nobel Prize for Literature in 1979.

El Greco, the Painter

Born in the village of Fodele on Crete in 1541 (➤96) the painter Domenikos Theotokopoulos would spend most of his life overseas, becoming known wherever he lived as The Greek, or El Greco. An artist of immense talent, he studied under one of the greatest Cretan painters of the day, Michael Damaskinos. At the age of 27, Theotokopoulos moved to Venice to further his studies and pursue the art of icon painting. There he successfully combined the Byzantine style that he had mastered on Crete with the Renaissance style that was prevalent in Italy. After almost ten years in Italy with limited commercial success, he moved to Toledo, Spain, where he lived for the most part until his death in 1614. It was there he

> El Greco was a virtuoso of Mannerism

achieved fame as a fine sculptor and architect as well as an artist. Several of his paintings are in the National Gallery in Athens, but only two can be seen on his native island, in the Historical Museum in Iraklio (➤62).

Monument in Iraklio that honours Nikos Kazantzakis, El Greco and Vitsentzos Kornáros

Nikos Kazantzakis, the Writer

Crete's legendary writer Nikos Kazantzakis (1883–1957) called his auto-biography *Report to Greco*, in a nod to his great forebear. Born in Iraklio in 1883, Kazantzakis is forever associated with the character he created for his 1946 novel, *Zorba the Greek*. Widely regarded as signifying the robust Cretan character, Zorba was in fact a mainland Greek who came to Crete and showed the locals how to live. The author's ambivalence to his fellow islanders – he spent most of life away from Crete – is shown in *Christ Recrucified*, in which Cretan villagers tear each other apart while the Turkish rulers stand by.

Despite his conflicting emotions about Crete Kazantzakis was proud of the island. At his request, he was buried in Iraklio and his grave stands on top of the Martinengo Bastion on the city walls. His epitaph reveals much about the Cretan character: "I hope for nothing. I fear nothing. I am free."

The BATTLE of CRETE

The Battle of Crete began with the biggest airborne assault in military history. So determined was Hitler to capture the island that he launched an offensive on 20 May 1941 that turned the sky polka dot with planes and paratroopers.

In what was known as Unterrnehmen Merkur (Operation Mercury), tens of thousands of German soldiers invaded the island in an event that lives on in the mind of every Cretan through stories passed down from those alive at the time to new generations. Crete was a valuable strategic stronghold and the British prime minister, Winston Churchill, described it as his island fortress, believing it to be impregnable. And for some time the Allied naval forces succeeded in keeping German forces at bay.

Operation Mercury

At the time of the invasion some 32,000 Allied troops (British, Australian and New Zealand) were recuperating on Crete, having been evacuated from Greece and the Balkan countries. The Italian army had invaded the Greek mainland in October 1940, and with German help had pushed their way through the country, forcing the evacuation of troops to Crete. Crete's location in the southern Mediterranean, offering access to Greece, North Africa and the Middle East, meant it was tactically important. So in order to secure it, Hitler took to the skies in an audacious and dramatic move.

The Battle Begins

At 6am on 20 May the initial bombardment began. At 8am, after a short lull, another wave of planes flew over. And at 8:15am thousands of para-troopers began filling the skies, concentrating at first on Chania and the

important airfield nearby at Maleme. German losses were initially heavy as ordinary Cretans rushed to help the troops defend their island. Men, women and children, armed with pitchforks, old rifles and makeshift weapons killed many of the invaders before they had time to untangle their parachutes after floating to earth.

While the first day had not gone well for the Germans, their decision to concentrate on taking the airport the next day bore fruit and the sheer

The Magazine

A child's drawing of The Battle of Crete, displayed in the Naval Museum of Crete

scale of the attack proved too much for the Allied forces. After several hours of heroic defence the Germans seized Hill 107, a strategic position that enabled them to take control of the airfield. After this, German planes were able to land and bring in more troops and weaponry.

AN AUDACIOUS KIDNAPPING

British travel writer Patrick Leigh Fermor was an intelligence officer in the British Army, serving on Crete. After the German invasion he lived in the Cretan mountains for two years and, disguised as a shepherd, helped co-ordinate the Cretan resistance. In 1944 he was responsible for the audacious kidnap of the German Commander on Crete, General Kreipe (▶ 96). *Ill Met by Moonlight*, written by Fermor's fellow conspirator, W Stanley Moss, tells how the resistance fighters succeeded in kidnapping Kreipe from the very heart of German headquarters, spiriting him away to the mountains and eventually taking him off the island to Egypt for interrogation.

It's an Enigma

German troops were also landing at Iraklio and Rethimnon, although it took them until 31 May to capture Rethimnon. By this time the Allies were in retreat, crossing the White Mountains, heading down the Imbros Gorge and evacuating to Egypt from the little port of Chora Sfakion (▶ 154). Cretan resistance, however, didn't stop with the withdrawal of the Allied troops. It continued courageously until the end of the war.

The battle was not only strategically important, it was significant because of Hitler's use of masses of paratroopers, the resistance shown by civilians, and the fact that the Allies were expecting the invasion, having cracked the German's Enigma code for encrypting messages. How the

...lies were defeated by the ...ermans after being forewarned ...mains a controversial and often ...eated subject of discussion.

Several significant sights related ... the battle are the Maritime ...useum at Chania (▶ 139), the ...onastery Moni Preveli (▶ 152), ...e German War Cemetery in ...aleme (✚ 188 C4) or the Allied ...ar Cemetery at Souda Bay (▶ 156).

...osing the Battle, ...Vinning the War

...lthough Hitler had planned to start ...is invasion of Russia in April 1941, ...e decided instead to prioritise the ...ask of capturing Crete and thus delay ...he attack on Russia until June. ...Vhile taking Crete was important to ...itler, it may have been a decision ...hat cost him the war, because as a ...esult of the delay his armies had not captured Moscow or Leningrad ...St Petersburg) by the time the harsh Russian winter struck. When Hitler ...ordered his southern troops to attack Stalingrad (now Volgograd), a quarter ...f a million German soldiers were killed or wounded, a defeat from which ...itler's army never fully recovered. Though they lost the Battle of Crete, ...he Allies went on to defeat the Germans and win the war.

CASUALTIES

Official casualty figures necessarily include estimates and probably underestimate the numbers involved. Greek figures aren't known, but the German air corps recorded taking 5,255 Greek prisoners. The Allied forces reported 1,751 killed, with 1,738 wounded, and 12,254 prisoners of war. In addition, the Allied naval forces estimated that well over 2,000 seamen died. The Germans estimated about 4,000 men killed or not accounted for, and another 2,600 wounded. Countless lives were lost in the Battle of Crete, and many more during the 1941–45 German occupation.

◀ **The Allied War Cemetery at Souda**

EAT, DRINK and be MERRY

Cretan cuisine is as tasty as it is healthy, blending pulses, olive oil, fruit and vegetables, and fresh fish and seafood – all washed down with the island's robust red wine. The keys to Cretan cooking are seasonality and simplicity.

Fruit and Vegetables

The diet's strength is its emphasis on fresh vegetables and Cretans consume three times as many vegetables as other Europeans, with artichokes, tomatoes, cucumbers, spinach, aubergines, beans, carrots, potatoes and leeks all organically grown on the island. They also eat several times more fruit than other Europeans and you'll find fresh fruit offered at every opportunity – especially oranges, which grow prolifically on the island.

Fish and Seafood

The island's long, thin shape means that you're never too far from the sea and a supply of fresh seafood – and Cretans love nothing more than a seafood feast. You'll find swordfish, tuna, bream, sea bass, mullet, squid, whitebait and sardines on offer, all caught locally.

Cretans eat plenty of fresh fruit   **Delicacies from the Sea of Crete**

Olive Oil

Crete produces wonderful olive oil and it's used almost to the complete exclusion of other fat products. Crete's extra virgin olive oil tastes so delicious that it's almost a sin that it's so good for you.

Wine and spirits

You'll find wine on the table of almost every meal after breakfast in Crete, however, Cretans drink in moderation. The local wines, both white and red, perfectly match the cuisine. You'll also find two clear spirits offered in most restaurants and bars: *tsikoudia* (a brandy-like Crete speciality made from the residue of grapes used to make wine) and *ouzo* (an aniseed-flavoured aperitif).

THE CRETAN DIET

Research begun in 1956 by American nutritionist Dr Ancel Keys compared diets, diseases and death rates in seven countries, including Japan, Italy and the US. Greek studies were undertaken in Corfu and Crete, with Crete showing by far the lowest mortality rates for heart diseases and cancer. In Finland, for example, there were 972 such deaths per 100,000 people in 1986, whereas the figure for Crete was just 38, the lowest in the world. Dr Keys was so impressed by this data that he followed the Cretan Diet himself – all the way to age 100.

What to eat

Apart from regional specialities such as snails and rabbit, you'll find most taverna menus to be similar. Locals usually start with a salad such as the classic Greek salad (tomatoes, onion, cucumber, olives and feta cheese), followed by grilled fish or moussaka (aubergine and minced lamb casserole). The perennial favourite is *souvláki* (meat grilled on a skewer) of which chicken, lamb and pork are popular.

Wine is an important part of the meal   **Lemons are also grown on the island**

The Cretan
HABITAT and its
CREATURES

Crete's landscape – and its flora and fauna – has been changed considerably by human habitation. As you explore the island today, it's still possible to enjoy breathtaking scenery and sight some spectacular creatures.

The Heart-stopping Cretan Habitat

Crete's defining natural features are its spectacular mountains, covering two-thirds of its surface. Four colossal limestone ranges dominate the centre from the east coast to the west. The highest and most dramatic are the Lefka Ori, or White Mountains, in the west; the central Psiloritis range (➤ 97), with the highest peak; and in the east, the Dikti and Sitia ranges (➤ 118).

Carved into the mountains are some awe-inspiring gorges. Samaria is Crete's most famous gorge (➤ 146), but others also offer rewarding – and less crowded – hikes, such as the Imbrou Gorge, northeast of Chora Sfakion (➤ 154); Kotsifou Gorge, north of Plakias; Kourtaliotiko Gorge, north of Moni Preveli; and Aradena Gorge, west of Loutro.

THE FACTS

Surface area: 8,300km²/3,200mi².

Length east to west: 250km/155mi.

Width north to south: 60km/37mi (widest), 12km/7mi (narrowest).

Highest peak: Mount Ida (Psiloritis), 2,456m/8,060ft.

Longest gorge: Samaria, 8km/11mi.

Longest river: Geropotamos, on the Mesara Plain, 45km/30mi.

Plundered Forests

Looking at Crete's landscape today, often covered in stubby kermes oak and *phrygana* (a low scrub), it's hard to imagine the whole island was once densely forested with cedar and cypress. The seafaring Minoans were the first to fell trees – using the timber for ships and buildings – and the Venetians and Turks continued the deforestation. Today only pockets of native woodland exist.

Along the tree line (1,650m/5,414ft) of the southern White Mountains are cypresses over 1,000 years old. Not only are they among the oldest trees in Europe but early signs of coppicing suggest they may also be the world's oldest managed forest.

The Magazine

Colourful and Aromatic

Growing wild on many hillsides are aromatic herbs such as oregano, thyme, sage, and marjoram and you'll often see locals gathering these herbs. Cretan dittany, or *díktamo*, is a medicinal herb that grows in remote gorges, used in ancient times to heal arrow wounds and ease childbirth pains.

In spring the countryside is ablaze with colour as wildflowers bloom in every field and crevice. One third of Greece's 5,752 plant species are found on Crete, of which nine per cent are endemic. One of the more unusual is *Phoenix theophrasti*, a native date palm (➤ 125). Several dozen African and Asiatic species, as well as plants from the Balkans and Western Europe, can also be found here. Above all, Crete is renowned for its wild orchids – there are some 67 varieties growing on the island – and bulbs, including wild tulips, Cretan iris and Cretan ebony.

Some of its Creatures

Sadly, with the loss of its natural forest habitat, Crete's deer and many other larger woodland species of mammal largely died out, but the small hardy, endemic Cretan spiny mouse (with its characteristic back spines) remains notable.

Another animal you may see is the *krí-krí*, sometimes called *agrími*, a large wild goat with sweeping horns much like those of an ibex. Its summer coat is reddish-brown, and males have a rather large beard. Once plentiful,

View over the fertile Lasithiou Plateau

The sure-footed Cretan wild goat

it was often depicted in Minoan art but was hunted to near extinction. The only natural population left is in remote areas of the White Mountains and the Samaria Gorge (► 146).

Crete's geographical position and diverse habitats of high coastal cliffs, rocky islets, wetlands and meadows make it a mecca for birdlife. Out of Greece's 420 species, 350 have been spotted on Crete, and the island is also a stopover for winter migrants.

Crete is the last breeding ground in Greece for the rare and endangered lammergeier, or bearded vulture. This magnificent bird has a wingspan up to 3m (10ft). Only a few breeding pairs remain but the vulture is occasionally spotted above the Omalos or Lasithiou plateaux (► 168). You are more likely to spot the more common griffon vulture, with its distinctive white head.

Endangered Species

The Cretan wildcat, *fourokattos* (furious cat), was assumed to be a myth until a team studying carnivorous animals accidentally trapped this elusive, nocturnal animal in 1996. Weighing 5.5kg (12lb), with a tawny coat and tiger-like growl, it's not in fact related to the cats of mainland Greece or Europe but to a North African species.

The beaches west of Rethimnon, west of Chania and around Matala are important breeding grounds for the loggerhead sea turtle. The Sea Turtle Protection Society of Greece (www.archelon.gr) operates a conservation programme, with kiosks at these resorts to raise public awareness. Most in danger of extinction, though, is the Mediterranean monk seal, which has been seen around islets off the coast.

ICONS
of Their Time

Icon painting is a great Cretan tradition and the island's artists became renowned for the genre from the 15th to 17th centuries under the name of the Cretan School.

Icons were being painted for many centuries before this, of course, but during that period Cretan artists were in great demand in Venice, the artistic capital of the western world. The Cretan School reached a peak around the Fall of Constantinople in 1453, with many artists relocating to Crete and the island became a centre for the art.

The icon painting of the Cretan School was renowned for the balance of the compositions, the strong use of colour in the garments of the subjects and the sharp lines of the brushstrokes. The School's fame spread widely throughout the 16th century and the painters organised themselves into guilds. A master of one was no less than El Greco (► 24) – at the ripe old age of 22.

Painters in the Cretan School were often versatile, being able to paint *alla greca*, in the Byzantine style, as well as *alla latina*, referring to the Renaissance style that El Greco later became famous for.

A Skill for Today

Today icon painting is a skill that is still highly respected on Crete, though few artists today create icons in the traditional way. The frame for an icon painting must be made from a hard, dry wood like oak, chestnut or pine, not an oily wood such as the olive tree. The paper is handmade from cotton.

An artist continues the tradition of icon painting on Crete

A fine example of Cretan icon art

Egg and vinegar are used to make the egg tempura, and 23-carat gold leaf provides the background. Paints are also handmade in the traditional way, with dyes derived from minerals, plants and metals.

The best place to see the classic icon paintings is at the Icon Museum in Iraklio (➤ 64). If you're inspired to buy or commission a new icon painting, make sure that the painter is using traditional methods.

Insider Tip

FESTIVALS

Cretans love a festival. There are public and religious holidays, Saints' Days, and festivals devoted to arts, culture, wine, sultanas – and even potatoes!

January
6 January: Feast of the **Epiphany** and Blessing of the Waters celebrated in ports.

February/March
Carnival celebrated around Crete with street parties 40 days before Easter, notably in Sitia and Rethimnon.

March/April
Good Friday: solemn street processions, mostly in the evening but in some places also during the day.
Easter: almost all Cretans attend midnight mass on Saturday night, followed by fireworks, crackers and bonfires (dates: 11 April 2015, 30 April 2016).

May/June
Matala Festival: open-air festival on Matala beach on the south coast, featuring Cretan and international music that pays tribute to its past as a hippie haven.

Summer
Summer festivals around Crete, notably Iraklio's Summer Arts Festival, Sitia's cultural festival Kornaria, and Rethimnon's Cretan Diet Festival and Renaissance Festival.

Ins Tip

August
Mid-August: Sitia **Sultana Festival**, involving much imbibing and feasting. **Potato Festival,** in Tzermiado on the Lasithiou Plateau, is rich in tradition.
25 August: **Feast of Agios Titos**, Crete's patron saint, celebrated across Crete.

October
28 October: **Ochi Day**, celebrated throughout Greece, commemorating Greek General Metaxas' one-word response *ochi* (no) to Mussolini's request to allow Italian troops into Greece in 1940.

December
6 December: **Feast of Agios Nikolaos**, patron saint of seafarers, celebrated in Agios Nikolaos (► 112) and around Crete.

Finding Your Feet

Finding Your Feet

First Two Hours

Arriving

The two main points of entry are both on the north coast of Crete. Iraklio, the capital, serves the centre and east of the island and Chania, the second city, serves the west. Both have ferry ports and international airports Iraklio is served by more airlines and ferries so may be more convenient from that point of view, but if your main interest is in visiting the west of Crete, try to arrange to arrive at Chania.

A third airport capable of taking international flights is at Sitia. It would be worth checking flights here if you wish to visit the less busy eastern end of the island.

It takes about two hours to drive the 160km (100mi) between Iraklio and Chania along the good New Road (National Highway), which runs for most of the length of Crete's north coast. While most visitors to Crete organise a rental car, which they tend to pick up and drop off at the airport, there is also a good bus service between the two cities and they are both major centres for the extensive bus network, making it fairly easy and inexpensive to get around the island.

Iraklio Airport

- The airport is **5km (3mi) east of the city centre** (open 24 hours a day; tel: 2810397800; www.heraklion-airport.heraklion-crete.org).
- **Bus No 1** leaves from in front of the terminal for the city centre every few minutes from 6am to 11pm. The fare is about €1.50.
- **Numerous taxis** can always be found outside the airport. Check that the fare is **metered** and the meter switched on, or agree the fare beforehand. Take time to find the board at the taxi rank that lists the approximate fares to most popular destinations (another reason not to go with a tout). A **taxi into Iraklio** should cost about €15 (higher after midnight) with a small charge for baggage.
- **ATMs, car-rental offices**, plenty of **luggage trolleys**, **shops**, **bars** and **cafés** are available at the airport.

Insider Tip

- Free **WiFi** is available in Café Cooking, upstairs in the international departures hall, while the Everest café has three public computers with free internet access.
- If you are **renting a car**, the airport is close to the New Road. Follow signs for Agios Nikolaos if you are heading east, or for Iraklio and then Rethimnon if heading west. Iraklio city centre is about a 15-minute drive away.
- If you need to **park** at the airport for any length of time, use the large and inexpensive public car park directly opposite the terminal building.
- Be sure to arrive at the airport at least two hours before your **departure** time as there are invariably long queues at the counters.
- Bear in mind that security regulations prohibit passengers from carrying **liquids** in their hand luggage.
- Unfortunately **delays** are common in summer on charter flights. There is far more room on land-side than air-side, so don't go through passport control until you need to. Summer is a very busy time, so give yourself at least 30 minutes to get through airport security.

Chania Airport

- The airport is **near Souda**, about 15km (9mi) northeast of the city centre (tel: 2 8210083800; www.chania-airport.com).

- **Public buses** run sporadically in Chania so you will in all likelihood need to take a taxi.
- **Taxis** are numerous and a ride into the city centre should cost about €15, more with baggage.
- **ATMs**, car-rental desks, shops and cafés are all available at the airport.
- If you are **renting a car**, follow signs for Souda to reach the New Road and avoid central Chania; otherwise follow signs for Chania to reach the city centre. When you reach the New Road, turn left to head east marked Rethimnon and Iraklio and turn right to head west. This is marked Chania but bypasses the city centre.

Sitia Airport

- The airport is about **2km (1mi) northwest of the centre** (tel: 28 43 02 44 24; www.sitia-airport.com).
  Taxis meet incoming flights. The fare into Sitia should be about €10.

Iraklio Harbour

- The commercial harbour lies about **1.5km (1mi) to the east** of the town centre.
- Numerous **taxis** meet the incoming ferries and **buses** going into the city centre, and to the regional bus station, stop on the main road in front of the harbour terminal.
- For **information** contact the Port Authority (tel: 28 10 24 49 56).

Chania Harbour

- **Ferries** dock at the harbour near Souda, which is about a 20-minute drive east of the city centre. **Taxis** and **buses** are available.
- There is a **daily ferry service** to Athens.
- For **information** contact the Port Authority (tel: 28 21 08 92 40).

Tourist Information Offices

Tourist offices can only be found in the large towns. They keep sporadic hours and are often closed during the winter.
National Tourist Office (Iraklio): Odas Xanthoudidou 1, tel: 28 10 22 82 03, opposite the Archaeological Museum.
Chania: Kydonias 29–31.
Rethimnon: Dimocratias 1, tel: 28 31 02 50 12.
Agios Nikolaos: I. Koundourou 21A, tel: 28 41 02 23 57.
Sitia: on the waterfront, tel: 28 43 02 83 00.

Getting Around

Travelling around Crete is easy provided you are not too ambitious. It is a big island, and if you want to spend some time relaxing then the best advice is to limit yourself to one region.

Bus

- Bus services are **generally good**. There are, for example, roughly 25 buses per day between Iraklio and Chania and a similar number between Iraklio and Agios Nikolaos.
- The **best services** are between the major towns and major tourist resorts.

Finding Your Feet

Buses here are usually frequent and comfortable. In more remote place you may find older buses in use, with a service restricted to an early morning bus into the main town, and an afternoon bus back again.

- Crete has two regional bus companies; namely **KTEL Chania-Rethimnon** that serves Iraklio and western Crete and **KTEL Heraklion-Lasithi** that serves Iraklio and eastern Crete. Bus station A in Iraklio is the central hub of both companies.
- KTEL is a cooperation of all the regional bus companies in Greece. Although they are regulated by the state the buses are owned by private companies or sometimes even by the driver.
- **Tickets** can be purchased in advance at the KTEL bus stations or you can purchase them on the bus from the driver or the conductor.
- Bus **timetables** are posted on the noticeboards at the bus stations and there are usually also printed timetable leaflets available. You can also see the timetables online at www.e-ktel.com/en/ (for western Crete) and www.ktelherlas.gr (for eastern Crete).

Taxis

- Taxis are a particularly **popular** form of transport among locals in Crete and are licensed to carry up to four passengers.
- All taxis are **metered** so you should only negotiate a fixed price if you want to hire the taxi for several hours for a round trip.
- There are **taxi ranks** but you can also hail a taxi from the side of the stree or make a reservation (for a small surcharge) with a radio taxi service.
- A special **night rate** applies between midnight and 5am and there are surcharge rates from ports, train and bus stations, and for items of luggage over 10kg (22lb). During peak times such as Christmas and Easter a surcharge of €1 is standard.

Ferries

- There are **numerous** ferry services, especially from Iraklio, to many of the other Greek islands. The only coastal ferry service is between Paleochora and Sfakion on the south coast.

Driving

- Most of the **main roads** are of a decent standard, the best being the E75 highway, that links towns along Crete's north coast. This is invariably signposted as the New Road, but is also called the National Highway (Ethniki Odos/E.O.).
- On many main roads and highways the **right-hand "lane"** is used for pulling on to when a car wishes to overtake.
- **Lesser roads** are often narrow with hairpin bends. It is best to to keep well in to your side of the road and to beep your horn before sharp bends.
- Never throw cigarette butts out of the car as there is an increased risk of **forest fires** on Crete in the summer.

Driving Essentials

- Drive on the **right-hand** side of the road.
- Wearing **seatbelts** where fitted is compulsory, but many locals ignore this rule. Don't be tempted to copy them.
- **Children** under ten must not sit in the front seat.
- **Drink-driving** is a serious offence. A blood-alcohol level of only 0.05 per cent means a heavy instant fine, and over 0.08 per cent can lead to imprisonment. The police sometimes set up checkpoints.

- The **speed limit** is 120kph (74mph) on highways, 90kph (55mph) on other main roads and 50kph (31mph) in urban areas. These limits may vary slightly so watch for the speed-limit signs.
- Drivers must give way to vehicles coming from the right, unless on a **priority road**. Many priority roads are unmarked and the only indications you will have are the right of way signs in the side streets.
- Be very aware of **motorcycles and scooters**, they routinely drive between lanes and weave in and out of gaps in the traffic.

Car Rental

- All main towns and tourist resorts, and airports, have several **car-rental companies** competing for business.
- **Rates** on Crete are higher than the European average, but local firms tend to under-cut the international names.
- The longer your car hire, the cheaper the **daily rate**.
- A **valid national driving licence** will suffice for most companies.
- **Minimum age** varies from 21 to 25, depending on the rental company's policy.
- Rental rates often include **third-party insurance** and **unlimited mileage**, but it is advisable to also take out coverage for CDW (Collision Damage Waiver), that is unless your credit card provides collision damage coverage.
- Rental companies **usually ask for a deposit**.
- Rental car insurance does not cover **damage** to the tyres and the under-carriage of the vehicle. This is done to discourage the use of the vehicles on unpaved roads or for off-road driving.

Bringing Your Own Car

- Cars can be brought into Crete for **up to six months**.
- EU citizens **no longer need a Green Card**, nevertheless it is best to have it with you when travelling.

Breakdowns

- Car-rental companies will **provide an emergency number** to contact.
- Members of motoring organisations such as the AA and other motor clubs receive reciprocal roadside assistance from **ELPA**, the Greek Automobile Club. You may need to pay for parts, in which case you should keep your receipt so that your association can reimburse you when you return home. The telephone number for emergency assistance on Crete is 1 0400.

Accommodation

This guide recommends a cross-section of places to stay, ranging from in-expensive but comfortable hotels to luxury accommodation. However, stand-ards of accommodation are generally quite high, and prices competitive.

Booking a Hotel

- It is quite common to **ask to see a room** before booking it.
- Online **hotel brokers** offer a large selection of hotels on websites such as www.booking.com, www.hotel.com and www.hrs.com. Some guarantee the lowest prices and they often also have cheaper cancellation terms than those offered by tour operators or the hotels themselves.

Finding Your Feet

- **Booking ahead** in high season is highly recommended.
- Travelling without pre-booked accommodation is **easier in spring and autumn**. Many hotels close in winter; if travelling between October and April arrange accommodation in advance.
- Many hotels are **family run** and are usually kept spotlessly clean. Facilities may be simple, but there should be everything you need.

Rooms to Rent

- In addition to conventional hotel accommodation there are also numerous other options such as **rooms to rent** (*domatia*) and small apartment complexes with studios (*diamerismata*) that have simple kitchenettes or apartments with fully equipped kitchens. These options are usually far cheaper than the cost of a hotel.
- There are no additional final cleaning charges for the studios and apartments and the landlord provides household linen and towels.

- The Guest Inn network (www.guestinn.com) offers a good selection of small guest houses and cottages away from the usual tourist resorts.

Rates

- All hotels are **inspected annually** by the tourist police, and the room rates and category of hotel agreed. These rates should by law be displayed in each room, usually on the door.
- Out of season it **may be possible to negotiate prices**, but don't expect any leeway in summer. Room rates vary according to the season and according to the standard of the room.
- The **price of breakfast** may or may not be included in the cost of the room, and this will be indicated in the notice on the door. The quality of hotel breakfasts varies enormously, from the perfunctory to the generous – and usually the cost is the same.

Tips

- When making your hotel selection, bear in mind that some so-called **beach hotels** are not actually on the beach.
- When looking at rooms be sure to take note of the surroundings. Some places may seem very peaceful during the day but come nightfall they are engulfed in loud music from the nearby **discos and outdoor bars**.
- Smoking is prohibited in most hotel rooms and any smoke will trigger the **smoke alarm**. However, guests are permitted to smoke on balconies and in other outdoor areas.

Prices
Prices are for a double room per night.
€ under €70   €€ €70–€150   €€€ over €150

Food and Drink

Greek cooking is delicious and Crete can compete with any Mediterranean island and hold its head high. The Cretan Diet (➤ 31) is one of the healthiest in the world, with lots of fresh fish, fruit and vegetables.

Specialities

Cretan cuisine is very similar to the cuisine served in the rest of Greece, but it is worlds away from the clichéd food in Greek restaurants abroad. Delicious dishes prepared with fresh, locally grown, seasonal produce, characterise traditional Cretan cuisine. There is a lot of home-style cooking, but also some creative, modern versions of traditional dishes.

- Cretan dishes are typically cooked a single pot, **oven baked** or barbecued on a **charcoal grill**.
  Pork and **beef** are the most common meats on offer as they are cheaper than lamb and goat, which tend to be more expensive.
- **Rabbit** is more popular here than in the rest of Greece, often made into a *stifado* (stew).
- Another staple, for those who can afford it, is **fish**. Fresh sardines, anchovies and other small fish are a popular treat with the locals and are usually served fried. Larger fish is relatively expensive and priced by weight. Make sure your fish of choice is weighed before it's cooked so there are no nasty surprises when the bill arrives.
- Two distinct specialities of Cretan cuisine are **snails** and pork that has been cured and smoked *(singlino)*.
- The nearest thing to a national dish is *dakos*, which is very similar to Italian bruschetta. In essence it is slices of oil-soaked bread topped with tomatoes, onions and feta cheese.

Eating Places

- There is a blurry distinction between **restaurants** and tavernas. Restaurants may be more up-market, and of course there are many smart restaurants in the major towns and tourist resorts. In a restaurant you will probably get a wine glass rather than a little tumbler, and a linen tablecloth instead of the paper variety.
- **Tavernas** are more down to earth, where service will be informal and you may be invited into the kitchen to take a look at the daily specials. The cooking in these family run affairs can be every bit as good as that in pricier places.
- *Psarotavernas* specialise in fish; *psistaries* feature grilled meat; and *ouzerí*, *rakadiko* and *mezedopoleio* are types of eateries that serve *ouzo* or *rakí* with plates of small Greek starters known as *meze* or *mezedes*.
- Fixed menus and one-course meals served with vegetables and potatoes or rice are only available in tourist restaurants. Cretans order their selected items individually, meat or fish, with vegetables and potato chips on a separate plate.
- When eating out with friends and family the food is served **family style**, with everyone helping themselves from large platters of food placed in the centre of the table.
- **Dessert** is often on the house and usually accompanied by a complimentary *rakí*.
- You should **book** in the more expensive dining places, especially on Friday and Saturday nights.

Eating Times

- **Breakfast** is usually served from an early hour in hotels, but cafés offering breakfast often don't open till about 8am.
- **Lunch** and **dinner** are both eaten late. Cretans have lunch from about 1 or 2pm onwards, although eateries open for business from the tourist trade from about noon onwards. In the evening, in busy resorts, some

places may serve food as early as 6pm, but this is only for tourists; in fact some serve all day, so you may not be quite sure if a table of diners is having a very late lunch or an early dinner.

■ **Cretans** don't dine in the evening much before 9pm, and truly local restaurants only start buzzing as it gets towards midnight.

The Bill

■ Bills usually include sales **tax** and **service charges**.

Drinks

■ Do taste the local **barrel wines**, made locally and sold direct from the barrel. The general standard is surprisingly good, although reds tend to fare better than whites.

■ Central Crete and the Sitia region in the east have some of the best **wine-growing areas**.

■ The Cretan national drink is *rakí*, also known as *tsikoudia*, which is very similar to Italian grappa. It is distilled from the pips, skins and stems of grapes used to make wine and does not contain any additives or anise.

Shopping

Crete may not be a destination that attracts people with its shopping, but nevertheless you will have no trouble finding souvenirs for family and friends. While most of the cheap souvenirs are mass-produced abroad. Crete still has a wide range of traditional crafts that are kept alive thanks to its popularity as a holiday destination.

Ceramics

■ The island has a wide selection of good quality Greek ceramics and there are numerous traditional **pottery shops** and workshops in the mountain village of **Margarites** (➤ 150) near Rethimnon.

Icons

■ Authentic icons made in the traditional way come at a price. The best place to buy them is directly from an icon painter; try the **workshops** in towns such as Iraklio and Agios Nikolaos.

Jewellery

■ There are **jewellery shops** all over the island but there are only a few remaining workshops where the jewellers produce original handcrafted work.

■ There are some very attractive collections of **museum replica jewellery** to be found in the jewellery shops directly across the street from the Archaeological Museum in Iraklio, and in the various museum gift shops.

Leatherware

■ Life in the Cretan mountains is tough, and sturdy leatherware has long been made for practical purposes. Today the workshops also produce **handbags, purses, wallets and other items** for the tourist trade, but you can still buy local items such as the long-legged Cretan boots.

■ **Chania** has the widest range (➤ 161).

Weaving
◀ This island tradition still flourishes, particularly in mountain towns such as **Kritsa** (▶ 116, 131), **Psichró** (▶ 131) and **Anogia** (▶ 96).
◀ Shop-fronts are festooned with **carpets and rugs**, far too many to have been produced by the one old lady who runs the shop. The better-quality handmade items will invariably be a lot more expensive, but worth it.
◀ **Chania** is also a good place to buy woven goods (▶ 161).

Woodcarving
For items of authentic Cretan provenance there are **olive-wood** workshops selling attractive carvings of bowls, serving spoons, breadboards and many other items.

Food and drink
◀ Both *rakí* and **ouzo** can be bought in elegant bottles that could be used afterwards as vases or shelf decorations.
◀ Almost all towns now have shops specialising in **Cretan herbs and spices**. **Cretan honey** is popular, being extremely pure and tasty, but is often far more expensive than at home.
◀ The real bargain is **olive oil**, as Crete produces some of the finest quality oil in Greece. Essential oils and cosmetics made with olive or avocado oil are also becoming more popular.

Entertainment

Arts and Festivals
◀ Art forms such as **dance and drama** are held all year round; however performances are held much more frequently during summer festivals. At these times, old forts and monuments are turned into theatrical venues. Iraklio (▶ 74), Rethimnon (▶ 162), Sitia (▶ 132) and Agios Nikolaos (▶ 132) all have their own local arts festivals.

Bars, Clubs and Discos
◀ Greeks traditionally prefer to do most of their socialising in the *kafeníon* rather than in the bar. In recent years, though, fashions have started to change. There are plenty of these chic establishments in the main towns, often crowded together in a laneway or a square in the centre of town, or lining the harbour, beach or seaside, and it won't take long to find out where the local action is.
◀ **Clubs and discos** are usually synonymous, and the larger resorts will normally have a few competing for custom. Some places such as Malia have numerous nightspots thumping out music till the early hours. Some have free entry, others charge an admission fee that buys you your first drink. Prices are not outrageously expensive, and most places don't get going till midnight. With a lack of listings magazines, look out for flyers on walls and telegraph poles telling you what's on where.

Cinemas
■ Cinema-going is a popular pastime on Crete and in many places summer sees the arrival of **open-air cinemas**.
■ Lots of **films** are shown in their original language with Greek subtitles.

Finding Your Feet

Outdoor Activities

- Thrill-seekers have a choice of two **bungee jumps** in Crete. On the south coast there is a 136m (446ft) jump from an old bridge into the Aradena Gorge and on the north coast there is a 50m (164ft) jump from a crane on the seafront in Limenas Chersonisou.
- Crete's only **18-hole golf course** is located in the hills south of Limenas Chersonisou and it is open all year round.
- It is possible to hire **bicycles** and **mountain bikes** in most of the resorts on Crete. There are also some companies that offer daily guided tours that suit all ability levels. Less strenuous are the tours that offer a shuttle bus up to the starting pointing in the mountains, so the cycle is mainly downhill.
- **Horse-riding** is a wonderful way of seeing some of Crete's remoter parts. There are several stables around the island, listed in the appropriate section.
- The best **tennis** courts usually belong to the large resort-hotels. Some are for guests' use only but others will let non-residents play on them for a fee, so it is worth making enquiries. There are public courts in Chania and Iraklio.
- **Walking** is one of the main reasons many people visit Crete. The mountains are spectacular and unspoilt, but even less energetic visitors feel compelled to take on the challenge of the Samaria Gorge (➤ 146). This trip can easily be arranged from any resort remotely within reach of the gorge. Travel agents will often also offer walking tours to less well-known places, such as the Imbros Gorge (➤ 153).
- **Water sports** are popular throughout the island's resorts and all but the tiniest of places have a water sports centre of some kind. Activities range from banana boats through to jet-skis, water-skiing and scuba diving, although the last is restricted to certain areas due to the fact that there are still many unexplored underwater archaeological sites around Crete. Many of the dive schools also offer introductory scuba courses for beginners.

Publications

- English **newspapers** and **magazines** are usually available in the cities and resorts by noon on the publication day.
- *Cretasummer*, free and printed in English, principally features life in Rethimnon but includes a few articles on the island generally, too.

Gay and Lesbian Travellers

- Chania has a **thriving gay scene** with a number of bars and clubs hosting gay events and dance parties although there are no especially gay resorts as there are, say, on Mykonos.
- **Gay travellers are as welcome** as any other travellers, and Cretans are as tolerant as other Greeks. The more outrageously dressed gay and lesbian couples will probably be looked at with amusement.
- Be aware of a borderline, though. **Overt behaviour**, which includes public kissing, goes a step too far and may not receive the same amount of tolerance.
- **Homosexuality is legal** throughout Greece from the age of 17, but you will not find many Cretans who flaunt it.

Iraklio

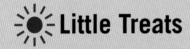 **Little Treats**

Even archaeologists make mistakes
The initial **reconstruction of a Minoan fresco** showed a boy; it is now seen as a monkey. Both are on display in the Archaeological Museum (►59).

Cretan jogging
Join the locals for an **iodine-boosting jog** along Iraklio's Venetian harbour breakwater (►60).

Panoramic views
Herb's Garden restaurant, on the roof terrace of the Lato Hotel, offers the best views of the city and its harbour (►69).

Getting Your Bearings

Iraklio may not be the most attractive city, but it is certainly vibrant and full of life. It is home to a quarter of the island's population. At its centre is the old town, parts of which are surrounded by medieval walls although – in contrast to Chania and Rethimnon – very little of the historical fabric remains. Wartime bombardments and the rampant building activities of modern Cretans have seen to that. However, there has been a shift in attitude since the beginning of the 21st century and new pedestrian areas have been established. Today the entire inner city between the harbour, Market Street and the Morosini Fountain has become an attractive promenade. This is also the site of the most important Venetian period buildings – mainly churches.

The starting point for city sightseeing tours is usually the long, sprawling harbour where the central bus terminal and the most reasonable parking places are also located. The old Venetian harbour, which is now only used by fishing boats and yachts, is the historical core. Standing here on the breakwater, visitors have a view to the south over the city with its hilly hinterland between the Psiloritis and the Dikti Mountains.

The central thoroughfare through the old town is Odos 25 Avgoustou, a pedestrian-only street that runs from the harbour up to the city centre. Most of the main attractions lie along this route, or on small squares near by. Odos Dedalou intersects with Odos 25 Avgoustou and leads to the Archaeological Museum. You can walk the short distance from one sight to another, and there are plenty of cafés and bars to stop at along the way.

Istoriko Mouseio Kritis ⑫

Platia Nearchou

Chandakos

Giamalaki

Michelidaki

Kalokerinou

Eka

Platia Ag. Ekaterinis

Agios Minas

Morosini Fountain on Platia Venizelou

⓫ **Frourio Koules**

⓫
Enetiko Limani

enizelou

rineli

Sof. Venizelou

Vironos (Byron)   Epimenidou

Platia
Koundourioti

Koroneou

neou   *Greco*
Park   Platia   **Agios Titos**
Ag. Titou ⓰

Malikouti

netiki
Loggia ⓱

Platia
Kalergon   Ag. Titou

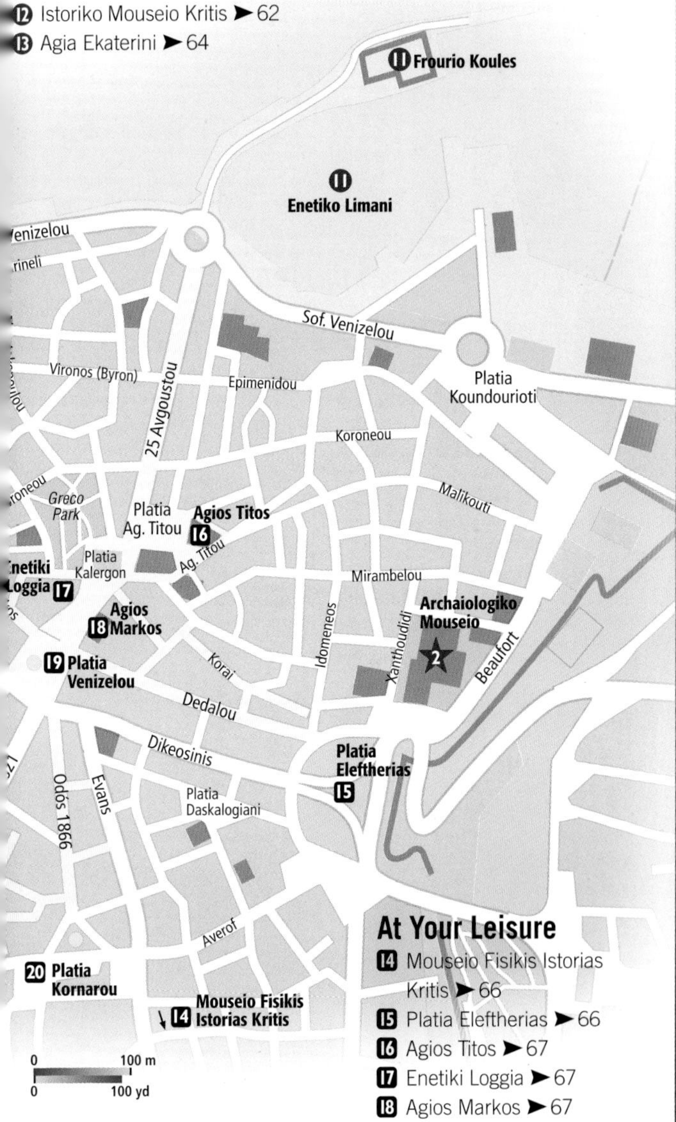

Mirambelou

Agios
⓲ **Markos**

Archaiologiko
Mouseio
★

⓳ **Platia**
Venizelou

Korai

Idomeneos

Xanthoudidi

Beaufort

Dedalou

Dikeosinis

Platia
Eleftherias
⓯

Odós 1866

Evans

Platia
Daskalogiani

Averof

⓴ **Platia**
Kornarou

↘ ⓮ **Mouseio Fisikis**
Istorias Kritis

0   100 m
0   100 yd

The Perfect Day

If you're not quite sure where to begin your travels, this itinerary recommends a practical and enjoyable day out in Iraklio, taking in some of the best places to see. For more information see the main entries (▶54–68).

⏰ 8:00am

Get an early start at the ⭐**Archaiologiko Mouseio** (Archaeological Museum; left, ▶54). The newly renovated museum was reopened in 2014. Set aside at least least two hours for your visit.

⏰ 10:30am

Walk down Odos Dedalou, the main shopping street, and turn right when you reach the end at Platia Venizelou. Continue down Odos 25 Avgoustou, stopping to admire the **17 Enetiki Loggia** (▶67). Just beyond, peek into the lovely **16 Agios Titos** church (▶67), set back on a small square with a simple café. You can sit under the shady trees and enjoy a second breakfast before continuing to the end of the street to the waterfront.

⏰ 11:30am

Walk out along the colourful **harbour** to the **11 Frourio Koules** (Venetian fortress; below, ▶60). Be sure to walk beyond the castle to join the locals on their popular walking route along the breakwater.

🕧 12:30pm
Have an early lunch by the waterside at **Taverna Paralia** (➤ 72), with lovely views of the fortress.

🕜 1:30pm
Walk along the waterfront to the **⓬ Istoriko Mouseio** (Historical Museum, ➤ 62) and then to the **⓮ Mouseio Fisikis Istorias Kritis** (Natural History Museum, ➤ 66), where you can try out the earthquake simulator.

🕓 4:00pm
Return to **⓳ Platia Venizelou** (➤ 68) and take a closer look at the Morosini Fountain. If you've got some time to kill, there's no better spot for people-watching. Have a rest at **Café Kirkor** and try Crete's traditional custard pastry, the *bougátsa*, or relax in the nearby El Greco Park.

🕖 7:00pm
Enjoy a cocktail at **Café Veneto** (photo above; ➤ 71), overlooking the harbour, before heading to a taverna on Odos Marinelli or to **Herb's Garden** restaurant in the Lato Hotel (➤ 69).

Frourio Koules ⓫

⓫ Enetiko Limani

Istoriko Mouseio Kritis ⓬

Enetiki Loggia ⓱

Agios Titos ⓰

Agios Markos ⓲

Agia Ekaterini ⓭

⓳ Platia Venizelou

Archaiologiko Mouseio 2

Platia Eleftherias ⓯

Platia Kornarou ⓴

Mouseio Fisikis Istorias Kritis ⓮

Iraklio

Archaiologiko Mouseio

Iraklio's Archaeological Museum is not only the major museum on Crete, it is the largest repository of Minoan antiquities anywhere and stands among the finest museums of the ancient world. This magnificent collection of pottery, frescoes, jewellery, ritual objects and utensils brings the Minoan world to life. Come here first, before visiting the ancient palaces and your view of the ruins will be enlivened with a sense of the colour, creativity and richness of the fascinating culture that once flourished on this island.

The collection of the Archaeological Museum covers 5,500 years of Cretan history, from neolithic times (5000–2600bc) to the end of the Roman era (4th century ad). The original two-storey building was built between 1937 and 1940. The museum underwent major renovations to extend and enlarge the building from 2007 to 2014 and it is envisaged that in 2015 visitors will be able to experience a modern, contemporary museum that showcases the island's rich and diverse culture.

A procession of figures on the sarcophagus from Agia Triada

Expect to see some of Crete's oldest artefacts, ranging from neolithic stone tools and crude idols to early Minoan pottery, figurines and jewellery from the Pre-Palace period (►Timeline panel). The ancient bull sports, later an important ritual in palace life, are represented by the small clay figures of bulls with acrobats grasping their horns. Look out, too, for early signs of Minoan craftsmanship in the

Vasiliki pottery from eastern Crete, with graceful, elongated spouts and deep red and black mottling obtained by uneven firing. Also noteworthy are the early seal stones (➤58).

The greatest highlights include finds from Knossos and Malia. The **Knossos Town Mosaic**, 25 colourfully painted and glazed earthenware plaques, depicts the remarkable architecture of Crete largest palace, as it would have looked in the 16th century BC.

The many human and animal figurines were votive offerings found in peak sanctuaries. Clay *taximata*, representing diseased feet, arms or other parts of the body needing cures, are forerunners of the silver ones pinned to icons in churches today.

There is a particularly precious collection of elaborate, polychrome Kamares ware pottery (also known as Eggshell ware), a sophisticated style of pottery with extremely delicate walls.

The style reaches its height in finds from the same period at **Phaistos Palace**. Large amphorae sport elaborate spirals, fish and other designs, while a royal banquet set includes a huge fruit stand and a jug with relief decoration of large white flowers. However, the highlight is the Phaistos Disc (photo below, ➤91) with its intricately carved hieroglyphic characters, possibly from a ritual text.

Some of the finest artworks date from the New Palace period when Minoan art reached its peak. These include

The Phaistos
Disc contains
many riddles

Iraklio

an exquisite gaming board from Knossos, made of ivory with gold casing and inlaid decoration of rock crystal and lapis lazuli, and two superb statues of the **Snake Goddess**, sacral relics from the temple in Knossos. Both figures are bare-breasted, one holding a pair of snakes in her upraised arms, the other with snakes coiled round her outstretched arms. They represent a major Minoan deity, or possibly a priestess engaged in ritual.

The famous Snake Goddess

The Bull's Head Rhyton from Knossos

Another treasure is the **bull's head *rhyton*** from Knossos (a *rhyton* is a libation vessel used in religious ceremonies). Magnificently carved from serpentinite, it has pupils of rock crystal inlaid with irises of red Egyptian jasper, and a mother-of-pearl muzzle. The original horns are missing, and based on the assumption that they were made of pure gold, the reconstructed ones are wood covered in gold leaf.

Other lifelike artworks that are equally impressive include the alabaster head of a lioness, also a libation vessel, from Malia; a stone axe-head carved in the shape of a panther, also from Malia; and the graceful ivory figure of an acrobat in mid-leap. The **harvester vase**, with its dark colours and natural patterns, is a new development in ceramic art. Clearly visible on the vase's bas-relief is a procession of farmers carrying harvesting tools. They are led by a long-haired man (possibly a priest) and are accompanied by several men singing along to a sistrum, a musical instrument.

Among the Late Palace period finds from the Knossos area is an interesting model of a Minoan house at Archanes and rare examples of Linear A script, the written language of the Minoans, alongside the Linear B script of mainland Greece. Among a range of objects from cemeteries at Knossos and Phaistos is a delightful clay statuette of men locking arms in a ritual dance between the horns of consecration, and another clay scene of ritual washing.

Equally famous are three elegantly carved steatite vases from Agia Triada: the above-mentioned harvester vase showing a procession of harvesters and musicians; the **chieftain cup** portrays an official receiving a tribute of animal skins; and the **boxer *rhyton*** depicts boxing, wrestling and bull-leaping.

MINOAN MOTIFS

Look for the major motifs that appear on artefacts from Minoan times: the double axe, the spiral and the horns of consecration were often painted or etched on pottery, while votive figurines took the shape of bulls, or goddesses with upraised arms.

Iraklio

This clay model shows a typical Minoan house

For many visitors to the Museum, the treasures from the **Zakros Palace** are pretty special. One of the triumphs of the museum is a stunning rock crystal *rhyton* with a green beaded handle, expertly reconstructed from over 300 fragments. The peak sanctuary *rhyton* depicts scenes of Minoan worship.

There should also be finds from settlements in eastern Crete on display, including the site of Gournia, from where there is a marvellous collection of **seal stones**. The Post-Palace period represents the decline of Minoan art, and the influences of Mycenaean Greece and Egypt. The museum's collection includes dozens of **clay sarcophagi** (coffins) painted with geometric designs. Many are shaped like bathtubs, and two are complete with skeletons. The limestone Agia Triada sarcophagus is considered the most beautiful of all. On one of the long sides is a depiction of a priestess sacrificing a bull while a musician plays a flute in the background. The other long side has two parts; one depicts two ritual double axes with two women pouring a liquid – oil, or possibly the blood of the bull – into a vessel. The other part shows men carrying two sacrificial animals and a boat to an armless figure standing in front of a ritual shrine.

SMALL IS BEAUTIFUL

Despite their tiny size, seal stones display an amazing degree of craftsmanship. Animals, people, imaginary creatures and hunting or religious scenes were carved in intricate detail on to hard stones such as agate or amethyst. These images were then impressed on to clay seals, which were used as a signature on correspondence or as a guarantee on shipments of goods. No two are alike.

The **Hall of the Frescoes** on the upper floor is another of the museum's highlights. Only fragments of the original frescoes survive (fallen from the walls and shattered into countless pieces long before being

discovered by archaeologists) but it is easy to distinguish the tiny pieces of original fragments from the paintings reconstructed around them. And we know that archaeologists can also make mistakes, one such example is the Saffron Gatherer fresco on the narrow side of the hall. It was initially thought to depict a young boy picking flowers but the figure was later reinterpreted as a monkey. In the middle of the hall, you will be able to see that not only the palace walls were painted: two sections of a painted floor are displayed in a low showcase. In addition, on the narrow side after you enter the hall, you will see that there were not only large format wall frescos but also small, miniature ones that could be used for decorating furniture and other objects.

The museum also boasts a superb collection of classical Greek and Roman **sculpture**. Also of interest are the decorative Roman floor mosaics with beautiful depictions of birds that were found in Chersonisou, while ancient trade is evidenced by the 30kg (66lb) copper ingots in the shape of ox hides dating to around 1450BC as well as the gold bars and pure gold ingots from the 9th century BC.

TAKING A BREAK

There are many cafés and tavernas nearby on **Platia Eleftherias**, while the bars and cafés of **Odos Korai** are also a short walk away.

✚ 187 F4 ✉ Odos Xanthoudidou 1
☎ 28 10 22 60 92
🕐 Mon 1–8, Tue–Sat 8–8 Sun 8–3
🍴 Cafés nearby (€) 🚌 Bus stop near museum
❓ No flash photography 🎟 €5

INSIDER INFO

Visit first thing in the morning, during lunchtime or in the late afternoon to **avoid the worst of the coach-party crowds**. Some of the rooms may be temporarily closed during 2015. There are plans for a museum shop and a cafeteria.

Must sees

- Phaistos Disc
- Bull's Head Rhyton
- Hall of the Frescoes
- Snake Goddesses

- Rock Crystal Rhyton
- Don't overlook the tiny gems, such as the seal stones, the honeybee pendant, or the ivory butterfly.

⓫ Enetiko Limani & Frourio Koules

Iraklio's Venetian harbour (Enetiko Limani) is one of its most attractive features, and a stroll around here with a visit to the Venetian fortress (Frourio Koules) that guards it is a relaxing treat. From the fortress you get an excellent view, not only of the city but of the remains of the Venetian shipyards, or *arsenali*, across the water.

Arsenali

Close up, the *arsenali* are none too impressive, surrounded as they now are by the modern city, but the view from the fortress shows something of their old scale and style.

Insider Tip

A look at the model in the Historical Museum (▶62) also helps re-create a picture of what life must have been like under Venetian rule. These 16th-century shipyards would once have resounded to the noise of large boats being built and repaired; today they are used for events and temporary exhibitions.

The graceful arches of Iraklio's arsenali

ST MARK'S LION

The winged lion of St Mark the Evangelist was the emblem of the Venetian Republic. It was depicted in all areas under the Republic's dominion, carved in limestone or marble above gateways or on public buildings and fortifications. Some 80 reliefs have been recorded on Crete.

Enetiko Limani & Frourio Koules

🎭 The Fortress

The fortress, which dominates the harbour entrance, was built between 1523 and 1540, though there had been several earlier forts on the site, one of which was destroyed in an earthquake in 1303. The Venetians rebuilt it and named it Rocca al Mare, Rock in the Sea, and the impressive name is appropriate for the building you discover beyond the entrance gate.

Inside, you step into a huge dark vaulted room with various rooms and

Today the Venetian fortress guards only the fishermen's boats

passageways leading off it. Ahead and to the right is a long steep slope that leads to the upper levels, where you can climb the walls for fine views of the harbour and city beyond, or out to sea. Some of the towers can be climbed, too.

The small fortress played a significant role in the 21-year siege of Iraklio by Ottoman troops. The siege began in 1647 and is one of the bloodiest in history. It was to last until 1669 and so also became one of the longest in history. Eventually the Venetians had to succumb, but only after a long and bloody struggle during which it is said that 30,000 Venetians and 118,000 Turks lost their lives.

The fortress has been extensively refurbished and some say it now looks more like a film set, but its scale remains impressive. It houses temporary exhibitions, and occasional plays and concerts are performed in the upper level.

TAKING A BREAK

You can enjoy good views of the fortress over a drink or a meal at the **Taverna Paralia** (► 72).

Venetian Fortress
➕ 187 E5
ℹ️ Closed for renovations but it is scheduled to reopen in 2015.

INSIDER INFO

- The 800m (0.5mi) long **breakwater**, which starts at the fortress, is ideal for a jog or a leisurely stroll.
- There is a small **fish market** held every morning at the start of the breakwater.
- Look for the **lions of St Mark** (see panel) above the entrance gate and on the seaward wall.

Insider Tip

⑫ Istoriko Mouseio Kritis

For an overview of the history of both Crete and Iraklio, a visit to the small but informative Historical Museum occupying an elegant Venetian town house is a must. Highlights of the collection include the study of Nikos Kazantzakis and two works by El Greco still on the artist's native island.

Insider Tip

At the ticket desk be sure to pick up one of the leaflets, available in Greek, English or German, which gives a map of the museum and a brief note of what is in each room. Most of the displays have information in both Greek and English, but in some instances the details given are fairly basic.

That said, in **Room I**, to your right as you enter, the information panels are anything but basic. They cover in some detail four of the major periods in Crete's history and correspond to four shelves of objects from those periods: the First Byzantine (330–824), the Arab occupation (824–961), the Second Byzantine (961–1204) and Venetian rule (1204–1669).

Forming the major display in this room is a wonderful 1:500 scale model of Iraklio as it was in 1645. At that time it was still known as Chandax, the name given to the city by the Arabs when they made it the island capital in the early 9th century; it may derive from the Arabic words *Rabdh el-Khandak* (Fortress of the Moat). On the walls beside it maps show the development of the city over the years; note the buttons beneath the displays that illuminate the relevant parts of the model.

The museum tour continues beyond the ticket desk, with the rooms spread over several levels.

Room II is the Ceramics Room and has beautiful bowls and plates imported from Italy during the Venetian period. These are cleverly displayed side by side with locally made pottery from the same period, clearly showing the Italian influence on local designs.

Lovely, delicate jugs and bowls from the Arab occupation of the island are also on display.

The rest of the ground floor has several rooms containing

A typical Cretan house, displayed in the Historical Museum

Byzantine items, Venetian coats of arms and carvings (note the fountain from a 17th-century palazzo in Room VI), with stairs leading up to the second level.

The highlight of **Level B** is undoubtedly the small, dimly lit room containing two inconspicuous small paintings by El Greco: the *Baptism of Christ* (1567) and the *Monastery of St Catherine Beneath Mount Sinai* (1570). Though both works are are unsigned, they have been attributed to El Greco. Signed works of the island's most famous son, who gained his fame in Spain, would be too expensive for Crete's museums.

The major display on **Level C** comprises the writer Nikos Kazantzakis's study when he lived

Memorabilia belonging to the writer Nikos Kazantzakis

in Antibes from 1948 to 1957, complete with manuscripts of his works, his library of books, and copies of his own books translated into many languages. It's an essential visit for anyone interested in this author.

The **second floor** of the museum contains a folklore collection based on the theme of the life cycle of birth, marriage and death. The museum's fine collections of weavings, embroidery, old costumes, household items, musical instruments and many other objects contribute to the display, along with newly acquired pieces.

TAKING A BREAK

While the museum does have a small **cafeteria**, one of the cafés on nearby Odos Chandakos may be a better option.

 Insider Tip

✚ 186 C5

✉ Odos Lysimahou Kalokerinou 7 and corner of 27 Odos Sofokoli Venizelou

☎ 28 10 28 32 19/28 87 08; www.historical-museum.gr

🕐 Apr–Oct Mon–Sat 9–5; Nov–Mar until 3

❷ No flash photography 🎟 €5

INSIDER INFO

- Don't miss **El Greco's paintings** and the scale model of the city.
- Cabinets in the centre of Room I, slightly overshadowed by the other displays, contain fascinating **glass and clay hand grenades** found on a galleon that sank in 1669.
- The **Emmanuel Tsouderos room**, opposite the Nikos Kazantzakis room, is unlikely to appeal unless you have a deep interest in Greek politics.

⓭ Agia Ekaterini

Icons are a way of bringing the saints themselves into the home, a door into a sacred and timeless biblical scene. As an expression of church theology and scripture, icons so often seem almost identical. However, under the influence of the Renaissance, an individual, freer style of painting developed on Crete. One of the greatest masters of the Cretan school was Michael Damaskinos and five of his masterpieces are exhibited in this museum.

The Icon Museum is housed in the Church of Agia Ekaterini, which was consecrated in 1555. It was once part of a monastery that included a theology and philosophy faculty and an icon painting school. The collection features icons created on Crete between the 15th and 18th century, frescoes rescued from Cretan churches and a collection of liturgical artefacts and garments.

Most of the orthodox icons depict the saints or biblical events such as the Annunciation, the Nativity and Passion of Christ, the Crucifixion, Resurrection and Ascension, and the Pentecost Miracle. One scene that is no longer common in the west is the ***Descent into Hades*** (▶ photo right). It shows Christ immediately after the Resurrection as He goes down into Hades, the realm of the dead. He is shown standing on the two doors to Hades that he has torn asunder and laid in a cross beneath His feet. He pulls Adam – as the representative of all mankind – out of the grave with His right hand. The Kings of the Old Testament are shown waiting to be reawakened to eternal life on the other side.

The five icons by **Michael Damaskinos** (1535–91) are considered to be among his finest works and they are the museum's greatest treasures. Damaskinos studied in

The Icon Museum is housed in the Church of Agia Ekaterini

Descent into Hades

the Agia Ekaterini monastery before leaving for Venice in 1577. He later returned to Crete by way of Corfu, which was also under Venetian rule at the time. His works form a perfect amalgamation of Byzantine and Venetian (Western) artistic traditions.

The strongest link to the Byzantine tradition can be seen in *The Ecumenical Council held at Nicaea, ad 325*; the major outcome of this was Arius being declared a heretic. The dignitaries are shown sitting in a semicircle around an empty throne and the true Gospel while Arius lies in misery in a small cave with his banned writings. By contrast, the *Adoration of the Magi* with an unusually large number of figures – including the three magnificently dressed kings from the Orient, their camels and a full retinue – shows especially strong Italian influences. Even further from the Byzantine tradition is the *Noli me tangere* icon, in which a Risen Jesus appears before a Mary Magdalene who is dressed as an elegant Venetian noble woman. This signals the final change from the Byzantine tradition to one with an increasing Western or Venetian influence. The other two icons by Damaskinos depict the *Divine Liturgy* – with the Holy Trinity and a large number of angels and saints – and *The Virgin with the Burning Bush* .

TAKING A BREAK

There are several **outdoor cafés** on the square between the Icon Museum and the Church of Agios Minas.

➕ 187 D3 ✉ Platia Agia Aikaterinis

INSIDER INFO

The Icon Museum has been closed for renovations for some time. At the time of going to press, it is expected to reopen in 2015. The tourist office opposite the Archaeological Museum will be able to update you on the current state of affairs.

At Your Leisure

Mouseio Fisikis Istorias Kritis

The museum, which falls under the auspices of the University of Crete, is housed in a protected monument – Iraklio's old electricity power plant – on the coast, west of the harbour. The museum is about a 15-minute walk from the harbour along a pleasant promenade.

The museum is really aimed at the locals and school groups so it is best not to expect too much. You will see some stuffed animals that are indigenous to Greece and Crete, photos of various Greek biotopes and a few fish in small aquariums. The museum also features temporary exhibitions. It is actually only worth paying the rather high entrance fee if you want to experience an earthquake once in your lifetime. There is an

Insider Tip **earthquake simulator** on the lower floor of the museum. It is set up like a classroom with sixteen stools around five school desks, after taking your seat there is a short introduction with information on safety precautions followed by 10 minutes of 'earthquakes'. The quakes are of varying degrees of intensity (up to 7.6 on the open-ended Richter scale) and a

Platia Eleftherias – "Liberty Square"

5-magnitude quake is simulated twice, so that you experience what it feels like on the ground floor and again on the third floor. At the end, you are given information on how to behave should you experience an earthquake in real life.

🚩 187 south of E1
✉ Odos Eleftherias Venizelou
☎ 28 10 32 46 61/28 27 40;
www.nhmc.uoc.gr
🕐 Mon–Fri 9–3, Sat, Sun 10–6
💶 €6

🅸🅵 Platia Eleftherias

Its name means "Liberty Square", and this large open space at the top of Odos Dedalou, opposite the Archaeological Museum, provides freedom from the sometimes claustrophobic feel of the city. This square was the centre of the city, and though the ring of rushing traffic around the edge has somewhat dampened its appeal, locals still frequent it for an evening stroll.
There are benches beneath the trees and and restaurants alongside.
🚩 187 E3

16 Agios Titos

Agios Titos sits back from the main road on a lovely square. With its sky-blue ceiling and dome, triple-tiered carved wooden chandelier and modern stained-glass windows, it has a light, airy feel in contrast to most of the churches you'll visit on the island. Built during the Second Byzantine period (➤ 22), it was the seat of the Metropolitan (bishop) of Crete. During the Turkish occupation it was converted into a mosque bu was rebuilt following an earthquake in 1856. Take a closer look and you will see the base of the original minaret.

When the Turkish population left Crete in 1923 it was reconsecrated to St Titus, Crete's first bishop. His remains had been kept here for 700 years until the Venetians took them to Venice in 1669. They were returned in 1966, and the saint's skull now lies in a gold reliquary under a wooden canopy in a side chapel to the left of the church vestibule.

➕ 187 E4
✉ Odos 25 Avgoustou
🕐 Generally mornings and evenings
💶 Free

17 Enetiki Loggia

After the fortress, this is Iraklio's second most handsome building. Built in the 1620s by Francisco Morossni, it was a place of meeting

and recreation for the Venetian nobility. Its Palladian style combines Doric order on the lower floor with Ionic on the upper. Medallions of famous Cretans decorate the ground-floor porch, with its elegant arches. The loggia forms part of a larger building that once held the Venetian armoury and now houses the town hall.

➕ 187 D4

18 Agios Markos

The Church of Agios Markos (St Mark), first built in 1239, was the church of the duke, ruler of the island. It became a cathedral in Venetian times but, like most other Iraklio churches, was converted by the Turks into a mosque. Unlike the others, however, it was not reconsecrated after their departure and in 1923 it became the National

The lovely façade of Agios Titos

Bank. Now restored, with a striking colonnaded porch and marble doorway, it is used as a concert hall and art gallery. The arched ceiling, fat pillars and stone walls of the interior make a superb display space for exhibitions of contemporary art.

Insider Tip

🔆 187 D4
✉ Odos 25 Avgoustou
🕐 No set times, but generally evenings
🎫 Free

⑲ Platia Venizelou

This small central square is one of the liveliest in town and a popular focal point for tourists and locals alike. It is named for the great Cretan statesman Elefthérios Venizélos, who became prime minister of Greece. Also known as Lion Square or Fountain Square, its centrepiece is the Morosini Fountain. Francisco Morosini, the Venetian governor of the city, built this regal work in 1628. An aqueduct, 16km (10mi) long, was constructed to bring water down from the mountains. The four stone lions supporting the central basin have great character and are even older; dating from the 14th century, they are thought to have come from another fountain. Carvings of mermaids, tritons and other marine figures

decorate the curvaceous marble base.

The square has plenty of cafés and restaurants where you can have a coffee, an ice cream or the custard-filled northern Greek speciality, *bougátsa*. The side streets off the square are also crammed with snack bars where you can get tasty *gyros, souvláki* skewers and pork tenderloin rolls, but if you prefer a quieter retreat try the nearby El Greco Park. It has pretty gardens and a children's playground at one end.

🔆 187 D3

⑳ Platia Kornarou

Iraklio's lively street market ends at Platia Kornarou, a small square that makes a pleasant place to rest awhile. The stone kiosk in the centre, which once housed a Turkish fountain, has been converted into a small café. Beside it is the Bembo Fountain, named after the Venetian commander, who first supplied the town with running water. It was erected in 1588 and incorporates the torso of a Roman statue from Ierapetra (► 123), about 65km (40mi) southeast of Iraklio.

🔆 187 D3

✪ FOR CHILDREN

A ride on the **Happy Train**, which follows the Venetian wall around the old city. Departures from the Archaeological Museum on the hour, 11am–2pm, and from the Venetian Harbour Apr–Oct 6–9pm; buy tickets on board (tel: 6 89 73 36 24).

Where to...
Stay

Prices
Prices are for a double room per night
€ under €70   €€ €70–€150   €€€ over €150

Atlantis Hotel €€€
The largest luxury hotel in the city is centrally located, between the harbour and Archaeological Museum, with only a short walk to most other city attractions. Its facilities include an indoor pool and an outdoor pool on the roof garden. The hotel was renovated and modernised in 2013.

🞖 187 F4 ✉ Ygias 2
☎ 28 10 22 91 03; www.theatlantishotel.gr

Capsis Astoria €€€
This modern hotel is right in the heart of the old town, on Iraklio's main square, just a few minutes' walk from the Archaeological Museum and five minutes from the Morosini Fountain. What makes it special is the terrific roof garden with swimming pool, bar and panoramic views over the city. Bicycles available for hotel guests free of charge.

🞖 187 E3 ✉ Platia Eleftherias 11
☎ 28 10 34 30 80-2; www.astoriacapsis.gr

El Greco €
The five-storey El Greco was completely renovated in 2013. It is centrally located in the heart of the city, on a very busy intersection, just minutes from the Lion Fountain and the market on Odos 1866. The hotel is, however, not recommended for guests with rental cars and traffic noise makes it difficult to sleep with the windows open. That said, it is better than average for a moderately priced hotel.

🞖 187 E3 ✉ Odos 1821 4
☎ 28 10 28 10 71; www.elgrecohotel.gr

Galaxy €€€
Situated in the newer part of town, about a kilometre from the centre, the hotel is best suited to guests with cars as there is plenty of free parking available. It has 127 comfortable rooms, a bus stop outside the door and plenty of amenities, including a big swimming pool and a gym.

🞖 192 A4 ✉ Odos Leoforos Dimokratias 75
☎ 28 10 23 88 12; www.galaxy-hotel.com

Kronos €
This clean, friendly, inexpensive hotel stands right on the waterfront road, which does mean some traffic noise at night in the front rooms. That aside, it underwent a complete renovation in 2011 and offers good value accommodation in the centre of town.

🞖 187 D5
✉ Odos Sofokli Venizelou 2, Agarathou
☎ 28 10 28 22 40; www.kronoshotel.gr

Lato Hotel €€
Many of its 70 modern, tastefully revamped (2012/3) rooms have lovely views of the Venetian harbour and its unassuming exterior belies its chic contemporary interior. Another major plus is that it has two great restaurants: a rooftop one for summer and a ground floor one for winter. Car parking is a 5-minute walk away, by the harbour.

Insider Tip

🞖 187 E4 ✉ Odos Epimenidou 15
☎ 28 10 22 81 03; www.lato.gr

Iraklio

Lena €

This modest 16-room hotel is conveniently located in a relatively quiet part of the old town, just five minutes from the harbour and the Morosini Fountain. A good budget option if you are only staying for a few nights.

🏠 187 D4 ✉ Odos Lahana 10
☎ 28 10 22 32 80; www.lena-hotel.gr

Marin Dream Hotel €€

Small, pleasant, mid-range hotel with 40 rooms. The rooftop garden restaurant, and some of the rooms, offer superb harbour vistas. Central location and very friendly service.

🏠 187 E4 ✉ Doukos Bofor 12
☎ 28 10 30 00 19; www.marinhotel.gr

Megaron €€€

This luxury hotel overlooking the Venetian harbour is housed in an impressive 80-year-old building that was once an office and warehouse. A health club and a rooftop swimming pool are a few of the indulgences on offer. It is also located within a few minutes' walk to the bus station and the Archaeological Museum.

🏠 187 F4 ✉ Odos Bofor 9
☎ 28 10 30 53 00; www.gdmmegaron.gr

Sofia €€

As the airport is only a 5-minute drive away, this hotel would make a good base for your last night's stay. Some of the car rental companies' return sites are even closer. The hotel has ample parking and a small swimming pool in the garden. For trips into the old town there is a bus stop that is a 5-minute walk away. However, due to its location you can also expect round the clock aircraft noise.

🏠 192 A4 ✉ Odos Stadiou 57, Nea Alikarnassos
☎ 28 10 24 00 02; www.hotel-sofia.gr

Agapi Beach €€

The advantage of this 320-room all inclusive hotel is its location: it is only 6km (4mi) away from the city centre and also lies on a beautiful sandy beach. There are three swimming pools, one of which is heated.

🏠 192 A4
✉ Neo Stadion, Ammoudara
☎ 28 10 25 05 02, www.agapibeach.gr

Apollonia Beach Hotel €€€

Standing just 10km (6mi) west of the centre of Iraklio, the luxury all inclusive Apollonia has its own beach and the local bus stops right outside the entrance. The 321 rooms, bungalows and suites, all with either a balcony or terrace, are spread around the large gardens and there are two outdoor pools, a children's pool and a heated indoor pool. Travel agents often recommend this hotel as a good option for families as it caters to children of all ages.

🏠 192 A4 ✉ Amoudara
☎ 28 10 82 16 02; ww.apollonia.gr
🕐 Apr–Oct

Candia Maris €€€

About 6km (4mi) west of the city centre but with a quick and regular bus service into Iraklio, the Candia Maris makes an ideal base if you want to explore the city but also enjoy the beach. Water sport enthusiasts in particular will feel at home here.

🏠 192 A4 ✉ Amoudara
☎ 28 10 37 70 00; www.maris.gr/candia
🕐 Mar–Nov

Grecotel Amirandes €€€

This exclusive luxury resort, with a large landscaped garden, outdoor saltwater pool and indoor freshwater pool, sets itself apart with its contemporary design and excellent sports and spa facilities. It is best to book your stay through a tour operator.

🏠 192 B4
✉ Gouves, Iraklio area
☎ 28 97 04 11 03;
www.grecotel.com/crete/amirandes/

Where to...
Eat and Drink

Prices
Prices are for a main course for one person, excluding drinks
€ under €15   €€ €15–€20   €€€ over €20

Brillant €€€
Iraklio's most fashionable restaurant is the place to head for special night out. The strikingly elegant room is particularly moody at night and the service is warmer than you'd expect from such a hip eatery. The food shines as much as the design. Order some fine Cretan wines, and let the chef impress you with his creative combinations of seasonal Mediterranean products. On weekends Brillant fills late with dressed-up locals, so book a table for 10pm to enjoy the atmosphere.
🚹 187 E4 ✉ Lato Hotel, Odos Epimenidou 15
☎ 28 10 33 49 59; www.brillantrestaurant.gr
🕑 Daily, lunch and dinner

Ladokolla €€
Opened in 2013, this typical *rakadiko* serves small portions of Cretan specialities, so over the course of the evening you sample a selection of tasty *mezedes*. It's also a good option for vegetarians.
🚹 187 E5 ✉ Marmeli 13/Platia Agios Dimitriou ☎ 28 10 25 63 91
🕑 Daily from noon

La Grande Trattoria €€–€€€
Despite its smart appearance with candle-lit tables on two floors, this Italian restaurant in the heart of the nightlife district has something for everyone. The extensive menus range from pizzas and pastas to house specialities featuring chicken, fish and veal. Many of the dishes have an international flair using creative combinations of ingredients that go beyond the usual Italian fare and the trattoria claims to have Iraklio's only singing chef.
🚹 183 E3 ✉ Odos Korai 6 ☎ 28 10 30 02 25
🕑 Daily noon–3pm, 5pm–late

Veneto €
Sit outside on the small terrace and enjoy one of the best views of the harbour, you can also opt just to have a few small snacks with your wine, ouzo, *rakí* or beer.
🚹 187 E4 ✉ Epimenidou 7–9
☎ 28 10 22 36 86; www.venetocafe.gr
🕑 Daily from 11am

Ligo Krasi, Ligo Thalassa €
This simple no-nonsense taverna with enormous glass windows overlooking the harbour may not be Iraklio's most attractive eatery, but it's one of the city's most popular. It makes up for a lack of looks with exceedingly generous portions of *mezedes* – the speciality being freshly caught and freshly cooked seafood – at unbelievably low prices. The place is packed throughout the day and night with locals, so service can be harried and staff may be abrupt, but they're efficient and if you compliment their food you'll definitely get a smile.
🚹 187 E5 ✉ Corner I. Mitsotaki & Marineli (opposite Venetian Harbour)
☎ 28 10 30 05 01 🕑 Daily, all day

Loukoulos €€€
With its lovely courtyard beneath a spreading lemon tree and bougainvillea, and views into the kitchen,

Iraklio

this stylish restaurant offers the very best Greek and Italian cuisine, with other flourishes too. The wine list is excellent and the service impeccable. One superb speciality is veal with a sauce of dried figs.

✚ 187 E4 ✉ Odos Korai 5
☎ 28 10 22 44 35 ⏰ Mon–Sat noon–1am, Sun 6:30pm–midnight

Odos Aigaiou €€

With a rather smart dining room inside graced by big picture windows, and an expansive terrace outside overlooking the port, this is a reliable year-round restaurant choice for a long lazy meal. The speciality is superb fresh seafood and the fish and lobster (when in season) are recommended. Choose the seafood from the display counter and they'll cook it to order. The menu includes traditional Greek dishes and pastas.

✚ 187 west of F4 ✉ Odos Aigaiou & Spanaki (opposite ferry port) ☎ 28 10 24 14 10; www.odosaigaiou.gr ⏰ Daily, all day

O Kyriakos €€€

The Kyriakos has been around for 50 years and is where visiting dignitaries tend to be taken. There is a relaxed outdoor seating area shielded from the street by lots of greenery, and a slightly more formal dining room inside with white walls and yet more plants. Service is very friendly and the restaurant prides itself on its range of good *meze*. Aubergines stuffed with feta is a simple dish but deliciously done.

✚ 187 F1 ✉ Odos Leoforos Dimokratias 53
☎ 28 10 22 46 49 ⏰ Daily noon–5, 7–1am

Pantheon €€

With outdoor seating on both sides of the covered side street, the Pantheon couldn't be closer to the butchers and the greengrocers of Iraklio's market. It serves plenty of conventional dishes such as chicken and moussaka, but take a look in the kitchen to see the day's more unusual specials, such as lamb cooked in a clay pot in the oven with artichokes and peas, or aubergine stuffed with lamb.

✚ 187 D3 ✉ Odos Theodosaki 2
☎ 28 10 24 16 52 ⏰ Mon–Sat 11–11

Syllogi €€

This modern café on Market Street is similar to an American-style deli. The area inside is stocked with local products while delicious Cretan snacks are served on the narrow street terrace and in the small courtyard at the rear of the premises.

✚ 187 D3 ✉ Odos 1866 26
☎ 28 10 24 07 77; www.sillogi-deli.gr
⏰ Daily from 9am

Syntages €€

In a handsome, blue and white painted house, in street behind Eleftherias Square, this elegant restaurant quickly became a local favourite only short time after opening. You can sit downstairs in the courtyard or the informal interior or upstairs in a slightly more elegant dining room. The décor features quirky touches, yet the focus is firmly on the outstanding Mediterranean food, from traditional home-style cooking to more refined dishes executed with creative flair.

✚ 187 E3 ✉ Odos Koziri 3 ☎ 28 10 24 13 78
⏰ Mon–Sat 1pm–midnight, Sun 1pm–5pm

Taverna Paralia €

Set right on the waterfront, the Paralia's tables look out over the occasionally crashing waves and across to the fortress. On breezy days you can choose the sheltered seating indoors. The menu includes many standard Greek dishes, plus pasta and pizza, but the speciality is fresh fish, simply grilled.

✚ 187 D5 ✉ Odos Venizelou 5
☎ 28 10 28 24 75
⏰ Apr–Oct daily 10am–midnight

Insider Tip

Where to...
Shop

If you're after traditional crafts you'll find more choice elsewhere on the island. That said, Iraklio can offer a selection of all Crete's popular souvenirs.

Odos Dedalou, a pedestrianised thoroughfare, is the main tourist shopping street. These days it's mainly given over to fashion, with names such as Hugo Boss, Zara for men and women, Timberland, Nautica, and some shoe shops. The more touristy shops are towards the top end of the street, approaching the Archaeological Museum.

For unique Cretan gifts, try **Galerie Dedalou** at No 11, where you'll find replica coins and Byzantine crosses, repro watches, jewellery, silverware, icons and worry beads.

Aerakis (Platia Korai 14, www.aerakis.net) specialises in contemporary and traditional Cretan and Greek music; they also produce high quality recordings for their own record label.

In Iraklio you are especially likely to see gold and silver jewellery with Minoan motifs, or replicas of famous pieces such as the honeybee pendant from the museum. Shops opposite the Archaeological Museum have a fine selection.

You could also try **Vassilakis** at 28 Odos 25 Avgoustou, a family-run shop with good prices.

Kassotakis jewellery workshop, 14 Odos Katechaki, specialises in historically inspired Byzantine and archaic jewellery.

The square opposite the Archaeological Museum is lined with shops catering for tourists, with pottery, statues, icons, decorative Cretan daggers and replicas of the Phaistos Disc. There are also many rugs, textiles and woven goods, but these are often imported or factory made. True handmade goods will have rough stitching on the back and are more expensive.

Although **Odos 25 Avgoustou** is mainly flanked with travel agents and car-hire companies, there are a few shops worth browsing for gifts. **Emika**, at No 15, has a good selection of wines from local wine co-operatives as well as gift bottles of ouzo, herbed olive oils in pretty bottles, Cretan honey and packets of herbs. Further up the street, next to the loggia, **Cretan Nature** has a similar selection of gift items, including olive-oil soap and creams.

The most colourful place to shop is the market (open weekdays) on **Odos 1866**, also known as Market Street, which is always packed with both locals and tourists. There are stalls selling fresh fruit and vegetables, honey, olives, spices, nuts, dried fruit and sweets.

 Insider Tip

Cheese shops will let you sample cheeses from different villages before you buy. This is the place to find Cretan wedding loaves – the wreath-like bread topped with flower decoration – for a kitchen ornament. One shop sells lace table-cloths and embroidered linens, and you can also buy sponges, T-shirts, leather bags, belts and sandals.

There is also a large market on Saturday morning near the bus station, opposite the port.

Odos Chandakos, behind Platia Venizelou, has some nice little shops with handcrafted jewellery and other gifts.

Busy **Odos Kalokairinou** is Iraklio's high street, with Body Shop, Benetton and other fashion and shoe shops. There are also shops selling embroidered goods along this street.

Where to...
Go Out

Nightlife in Iraklio is generally not the raucous affair you find in the beach party towns. If that's what you're after, head for the clubs along the coastal strip at Ammoudara, west of the city, the hottest club scene in summer, or to Chersonisos or Malia (► 121) to the east. Also note that while bars are open all day until late, clubs and discos don't start up until 11pm or midnight.

In the cooler half of the year the small nightclubs on Odos Bofor are usually very busy at night. The largest open-air club right in the city is **Envy** (Odos Sofokli Venizelou). It is a café during the day but come nightfall the local youth dance to the latest hits from the Greek and international charts.

Pagopoleio, behind the Agios Titos church (Platia Agiou Titou 1, www.pagopoeion.gr), often plays jazz music.

The **Platia Venizelou** cafés are ideal for people watching and make an excellent coffee stop opposite the Morosini Fountain. Off **Odos Dedalou**, Odos Ioannou Perthikari leads to **Odos Korai**, Iraklio's most happening streets and the heart of its nightlife. By day, locals relax at the chic cafés and bars; by night the lanes are crammed with young hipsters sipping cocktails. Each season the bars get makeovers and name changes, so just head to the one you like

the look of. The **Cuckoo Bar** has live rock music on Mondays from 10.30pm.

The bars on **Odos Chandakos**, running northwest of Platia Venizelou, see a more down-to-earth crowd at their terrace tables.

Traditional Greek and Cretan music is played on most weeknights (after 10pm) in **Sxolarxeio**, a small, inexpensive bar and café behind the Agios Titos church (Odos Agiou Titou, www.sxolarxeio.com).

Iraklio's summer arts festival is held from late June to mid-September and features Greek and international artists in music, dance and theatre productions that range from ballet to Greek drama. Performances take place on the roof of the **Venetian fort** or in the **Nikos Kazantzakis Open-Air Theatre** at Jesus Bastion (tel: 28 10 24 29 77, box office). In summer the latter is also used as an open-air cinema. In the town centre, the **Alpha Odeon cinema** at Platia Eleftherias shows English films with Greek subtitles.

Water sports enthusiasts can use inexpensive public buses to get to **Amoudara** and **Krateros,** two **city beaches** that are well-equipped for water sports.

There is a large bowling alley, the **Heraklion Bowling Center** (Leoforos Ikariou 11, tel: 28 10 34 44 14), while tennis, table tennis, chess and bridge are on offer at the **Iraklion Sports Club** (Odos Bofors 17, tel: 28 10 22 47 45).

Central Crete

 Little Treats

Knossos from above
For a **bird's-eye** view of Knossos (➤ 80)
take the small road that turns to the left,
just south of the excavations.

One for naturists
There is a half hour hiking path that leads
from Matala (➤ 99) to **Red Beach**, where
bathing costumes are optional.

Holiday on an equestrian farm
Melanouri Horse Farm (➤ 104) offers
horse-riding facilities and some family-
friendly accommodation.

Central Crete

Getting Your Bearings

Central Crete is the most densely populated region of the island – as it was during the Minoan era – and the site of the impressive palaces of Knossos and Phaistos. Heading from Iraklio to the south coast you'll find a countryside of lush, gently rolling hills; the fertile Mesara Plain in the south has always been the island's granary. The landscape is dominated by a powerful mountain range with Mount Ida, or Psiloritis, as Crete's highest peak.

Central Crete claims the top attraction on the island, the ruins of ancient Knossos, but it also has smaller, equally fascinating sites. Phaistos, near the south coast, has an attractive setting overlooking the Mesara Plain. Here you can see the spot where archaeologists found what is perhaps the island's single most important historical item: the Phaistos Disc.

Making sense of Agia Triada

Those fascinated by history will also revel in two other sites close to Phaistos. One is the Roman site at Gortis, the other the Minoan villa of Agia Triada. Both gloriously demonstrate that small can be beautiful.

The mountain village of Zaros is a gateway to some wonderful walking, but central Crete is also ideal for those who want to combine history with sunbathing.

Detail from the dolphin fresco at Knossos

The south coast resorts of Matala and Agia Galini both have good beaches, good eating and nightlife, and make great bases for exploring the whole area. From south to north is little more than an hour's drive...or more like a week if you want to explore every nook and cranny.

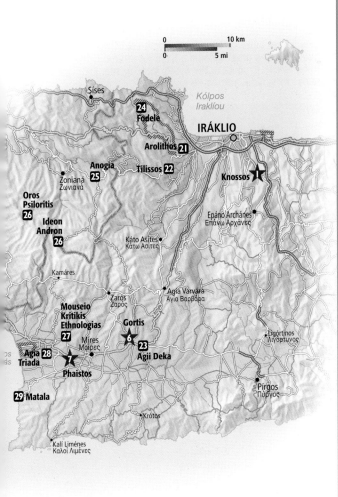

Top 10

⭐ Knossos ➤ 80
6 Gortis ➤ 87
⭐ Phaistos (Festos) ➤ 90

At Your Leisure

Three Perfect Days

If you're not quite sure where to begin your travels, this itinerary recommends a practical and enjoyable three-day tour of Central Crete, taking in some of the best places to see. For more information see the main entries (➤ 80–99).

Day One

Morning

Try to get to ★**Knossos** (right, ➤ 80) by opening time, to have any hope of beating the crowds and heat, and allow a good two or three hours at the site. Afterwards, head back towards Iraklio and take the New Road west towards Rethimnon, but turn off towards the craft village of **21 Arolithos** (➤ 95). The café at Arolithos is surprisingly good, but don't linger too long.

Afternoon

The ancient site of **22 Tilissos** (➤ 95) closes at 3pm so try to arrive by 2pm to enjoy it before continuing on the winding mountain road to **25 Anogia** (➤ 96). If time and daylight allows, continue on the Nida Plateau to **26 Psiloritis** and the **Ideon Andron** (➤ 97), though you should allow at least two hours.

Evening

Spend the night in **Anogia**, where there is a hotel and rooms to rent. A good dining spot is the simple Taverna Skalomata on the right as you leave the village on the road to the cave, which has great views.

Day Two

Morning

Drive via Zoniana (with its stalactite cave), and the picturesque village of Melidoni, to the New Road and follow it along the coast towards Iraklio. Take a break in the village of **24 Fodele** (➤ 96), the birthplace of El Greco, where you can go for a swim and enjoy lunch at Fodele beach.

Afternoon

Head back towards Iraklio on the New Road but as you reach the city look for the right turn marked to Mires. This is a fast road but makes a pleasant drive as it eventually heads up into the hills. In Agia Varvara watch carefully for the almost hidden little right turn to **Zaros**.

Evening

After another lovely drive, relax by the pool and later dine at the restaurant of the Idi Hotel (➤ 100) in Zaros.

Day Three

Morning

Explore **Zaros** (➤ 164) and go for a short walk up the gorge before heading south on the road to Moires, turning left to reach ⭐**Gortis** (photo above, ➤ 87).

Lunch

East of Gortis is the church of **23 Agii Deka** (➤ 95). The village has several authentic tavernas where few tourists venture.

Afternoon

Allow plenty of time for visiting ⭐**Phaistos** (➤ 90) before deciding where to spend the night: in the small resort of **29 Matala** (photo below, ➤ 99), or the bigger but prettier **30 Agia Galini** (➤ 99).

Evening

The **Lions Restaurant** in Matala (➤ 102) has excellent food, while Agia Galini offers numerous choices, including **Madame Hortense** (➤ 101) and the Onar (➤ 101).

★ Knossos

Historical wonder or archaeologist's fantasy? The Minoan palace of Knossos is Crete's biggest attraction, and its excavation yielded the most important remains of this ancient civilisation. Even if you find its reconstructed rooms and columns a travesty, they are none the less fascinating and help to make sense of the sprawling maze of stone. Unlike many archaeological sites, Knossos provides an intimate glimpse of the lives that might have been lived here.

Covering a vast area of 75 hectares/185 acres (only a portion of which is open to the public), Knossos is the largest of the Minoan palaces. It was built on five levels and had over 1,200 rooms, providing accommodation for a huge court. It is thought that more than 100,000 people lived in and around the palace when the Minoan civilisation was at its height.

The ancient palace of Knossos is Crete's biggest attraction

Neolithic remains found at Knossos suggest that there were settlers here as far back as 6000BC. The first Minoan palace was constructed around 2000BC, but was destroyed in an earthquake three centuries later. What you see today are the remains of the even grander palace that replaced it. Even after this palace was destroyed in the great cataclysm of 1450BC (► 17), Knossos remained an important settlement for newcomers to the island well into Roman times. Afterwards it fell into obscurity until a Cretan archaeologist, Minos Kalokairinos – coincidentally named after the ancient priest-kings – discovered the storerooms in 1878.

A Reconstruction

A few years later, a young Englishman, Arthur Evans (► right), became intrigued by the site and bought up the land, and by 1900 a full-scale archaeological dig

On the Royal Way at Knossos

was under way. In just two years he uncovered most of the palace area, but his hasty methods caused important information to be lost or poorly documented. Of greater controversy was Evans' reconstruction of parts of the palace, which he claimed was necessary to preserve and understand it. There was some truth to this, as the original pillars and beams had been made of wood and as he unearthed room after room, the entire structure was in danger of collapse. Evans incorporated original fragments into new concrete pillars and supports, and restored rooms according to how he believed they would have looked during the Minoan era. Later archaeologists have been highly critical of his romantic re-creations, but Evans' work does give visitors a glimpse of the splendour of the Minoan world, and a means to visualise the frescoed walls, ceremonial staircases and red pillars that supported this multi-storey complex.

SIR ARTHUR EVANS

At the entrance to Knossos is a bust of Sir Arthur Evans (1851–1941), excavator of the site. He was a man of many talents, working as a journalist and war correspondent before becoming director of the Ashmolean Museum in Oxford at the age of 33. Ten years later, in 1894, his job led him to Knossos for the first time and he became intrigued by speculations of an ancient palace buried here. Evans was a wealthy man – and a tenacious one. It took him five years to purchase the land from its Turkish owners. Though his autocratic methods drew much criticism, his findings rewrote the history of the ancient world. He was knighted for his achievements in 1911 and continued to work on the site until 1935, when he was 84 years old.

The Palace of Minos

Knossos, the most important Minoan palace, is a very vivid example of the first advanced civilisation in Europe. With an area of 20,000m² (almost 5 acres) and more than 1000 rooms it is also the largest palace of this unique culture. Archaeologists estimate that around 10,000 people lived in the complex and its surroundings in its heyday.

❶ **Throne room:** The central element of the room is the alabaster throne that is flanked by benches; the walls are decorated with frescoes of griffins.

❷ **Central sanctuary:** Cult figures found here indicate that this was where fertility deities were worshipped. The sanctuary was illuminated by torchlight and this, along with the double axe signs, would have given the chamber a unique atmosphere of sanctity. Underground vaults or temple repositories were also found here.

❸ **Northwest wing:** Cult rooms decorated with beautiful frescoes were located in the northwest wing.

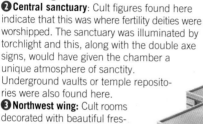

Pithoi were used to store olive oil and wine

Bull horns
are the most
common
symbol of
Minoan
civilisation

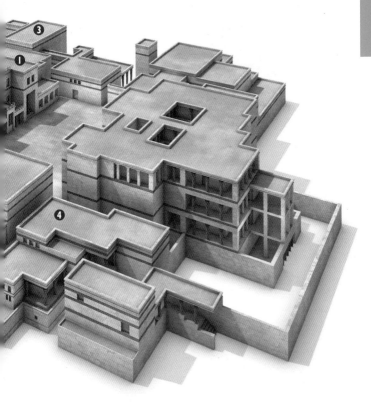

❹ Hall of the Double Axes: This chamber takes its name
from its double axe markings. The double axe was an
important object in the Minoan religious cult. This was
probably the official reception hall of the palace where
emissaries were greeted.

Central Crete

Seeing the Palace

With its narrow passageways, connecting rooms, raised walkways and Lshaped steps leading to dead-end landings, Knossos can be confusing. No wonder it has been linked with the mythical labyrinth of King Minos. Rooms are labelled, although they can still be challenging to find even with a map, but you will eventually come across all the interesting areas, sometimes when you least expect it.

Sadly, Knossos has suffered from its own popularity. The sheer number of tourists treading its ancient walls has caused structural problems, and many areas and paths are now roped off. False walkways have been built over the natural stone paths to cater for the tour groups on a beaten trail, but they spoil the character of the site and make it difficult for individual visitors to escape the crowds. The best way to enjoy Knossos is to take your time and use your imagination, or visit off-season.

Detail from the Ladies in Blue fresco

Insider Tip

WHAT'S IN A NAME?

The notion of Knossos as the labyrinth of King Minos may be more than just myth. In pre-Hellenic times the word *labrys* meant "double axe" and the ending *nthos* meant "house of" – thus, "house of the double axe". Giant double axes were found at Knossos, and were thought to be a symbol of power.

The entrance is through the **west court**, passing the circular pits where devotional objects were placed at the end of sacred rituals. Turn right, and follow the Corridor of Processions, where you first see the palace frescoes. These show a party of men and women carrying gifts and ceremonial vessels. Evans hired French artists to repaint all of the

WATERWORKS

A drainage system of terracotta pipes, ingenious for its time, ran below the palace and incorporated a means to stop or control the flow of water. You can still see parts of this system under grilles and around the edges of the royal chambers.

frescoes on site, once the originals were moved to the Archaeological Museum in Iraklio.

Inside the palace walls, on your left is the **south propylaeum** with its tapering white columns and fresco of a cup-bearer. On your right is a reproduction of the enormous Horns of Consecration, standing where the original fragments were found. Just ahead, in an upper chamber, is the famous fresco of the priest-king.

Evans gave the frescoes and rooms their names, such as the *piano nobile*, taken from the Italian Renaissance. A staircase behind the south propylaeum leads up to it, where there is a view over the central court and the store-rooms with their giant storage jars.

Below, in the northwest corner of the court, is the **throne room**, decorated with frescoes of griffins. The alabaster throne is thought to be the oldest in Europe. Opposite is a sunken lustral basin, used for purification. If you can't resist the impulse to pose for a photo, there is a wooden replica for that purpose in the antechamber. The throne room is one of the highlights of the palace and long queues often form as people wait to peer over the threshold.

The heart of Knossos is the **central court**, measuring approximately 55m by 28m (180ft by 92ft). Originally surrounded by high walls, it is where the bull-leaping rituals and athletic contests depicted in the frescoes took place.

The colourful griffin frescoes of the Throne Room

On the east side of the court, the grand staircase leads down to what Evans believed were the **royal chambers**. This is now also blocked off, but you can descend via a

The Dolphin Fresco adorns the Queen's chamber

corridor to your left. These are the best-preserved rooms, and though they are built into the slope of a hill, they are lit by a system of large light wells. Look for the king's chamber, whose ante-room is marked with shields and the sign of the double axe. The queen's chamber has a delightful fresco of dolphins. Sadly, the adjacent rooms, which held a clay bathtub and flush toilet, are no longer on view.

To the north of the royal chambers are the **palace workshops** and the magazines of giant storage jars (*pithoi*), used to store olive oil and wine. A **theatre** with some 500 seats lies northwest of the palace. The royal road, with original paving stones dating from the third millennium BC, leads north and may once have run all the way to the sea.

TAKING A BREAK

For a bite to eat it is best to swap the tourist traps of Knossos for a **taverna** in Iraklio or Archanes, where your will have a tastier and less expensive meal.

➕ 192 A4
✉ 5km (3mi) south of Iraklio on Odos Knosou
☎ 28 10 23 19 40
🕐 Apr–Oct daily 8–8; Nov–Mar Tue–Sun 8:30–3
🚌 Bus 2, 4 💶 €6

INSIDER INFO

■ Knossos is Crete's most popular attraction and it is always busy, especially in summer. **To avoid the worst of the crowds**, try to be there when the site first opens in the morning, or in the early evening. Midday can also be quieter, when large tour groups leave for lunch. The best time to visit is off-season

■ The **summer heat** is intense and there is little shade; bring water and a hat.

■ Allow two hours to **see the highlights**, more if it is very crowded.

Insider Tip
■ If the site's free parking area is full, you'll find **pay-parking areas** on the main road just before Knossos and immediately past the entrance.

⑥ Gortis

On an island full of Minoan remains, the ruins of this ancient Greco-Roman city give a glimpse of a later era. The core site is small but impressive, with the enormous basilica of Agios Titos and the law code – the first such code to be written down in Europe – inscribed on massive stone blocks. If time allows, you can wander through the surrounding fields and olive groves to discover the scattered remnants of this important city.

Spring flowers adorn the fields around Agios Titos at Gortis

The settlement of Gortis dates back to Minoan times. Built along the River Letheos (also known as the Mitropolitanos) on the fertile Mesara Plain, it prospered and grew under the Dorian Greeks and by the 8th century BC had become the most important city in southern Crete. When the Romans conquered the island in 67BC, they made Gortis the capital of their province Cyrenaica, which encompassed not only Crete but much of North Africa. A century later, St Titus (► 88) made his base here and set about converting the population – which numbered some 30,000, the largest on Crete – to Christianity. It became the religious as well as the political centre of the island.

Gortis flourished throughout Byzantine times until Saracen raiders sacked the city in AD824. It never recovered and was soon abandoned. Today its ruins cover a large area, much of which has not yet been excavated.

Agios Titos

The major ruins of Gortis lie within a fenced site on the north side of the road. As you enter, the massive shell of Agios Titos draws you to the left. Built in the 6th century,

Central Crete

it is the best-preserved early Christian church on Crete, and was the seat of the archbishops until the Arab invasion. The vaulted central apse gives you an idea of its former magnificence, and there is a small shrine in one of the side aisles. The holy relics of St Titus were kept here until 962, when they were moved to a new church in Iraklio (➤ 67). A service is held here once a year on 23 December, the saint's feast day.

The Law Code
Beyond the church is an area thought to be the ancient agora, or forum. Here, overlooking the remains of the Roman *odeon* (a small theatre used for musical performances and poetry recitals), is a building sheltering Gortis's greatest find: the law code. Carved by the Dorian Greeks around 500BC on to massive stone blocks, it represents the earliest known written laws in Europe.

The tablets are arranged in 12 columns standing 3m (10ft) high. The 600 lines of archaic inscription are read alternately left to right and right to left – a style known as *boustrophedon*, a word which describes the pattern made by an ox plough. They provide invaluable insight into this period of Greek history, particularly its social organisation.

Gortis's code of law, in clear detail

The code is actually a series of rulings clarifying laws that pertain to marriage, divorce, adoption, property and rights of inheritance. It also laid down penalties for adultery, rape, assault and other offences. Gortis's population was divided into a hierarchy of rulers, citizens or freemen, serfs and slaves, and the rights and penalties varied greatly among the classes.

The Acropolis and the Roman City
On the opposite bank of the river you can see the remains of a larger theatre. Above, on the hilltop, are the ancient acropolis and the ruins of a Greek temple, a Roman hall (the *kastro*) and ramparts.

INSIDER INFO

- It's a **steep, hot climb** to the top of the acropolis, but you'll get a great overview of the site.
- Near the Temple of Apollo Pythios is a small **Roman theatre**, the best preserved on Crete.
- You can easily skip the **amphitheatre** and **stadium**, both southeast of the *praetorium*.

Insider Tip

Dotted throughout the open fields on the south side of the main road, stretching back to Agii Deka, are various remains of the Roman city. Many are little more than scant walls and piles of stone, but it's good fun to seek them out in this atmospheric setting among giant gnarled olive trees. Several of the main sites lie along a track, including the **Temple of Isis and Serapis**, dedicated to the Egyptian gods. To the south, the **Temple of Apollo Pythios** with its stepped monumental altar was the main place of worship in pre-Roman times. To the east is the *praetorium*, the Roman **governor's palace**. Through the fence you can see its paved courtyards, carved columns and capitals and brickwork walls, and the *nymphaeum*, or bath suite.

TAKING A BREAK

On site is an unremarkable but adequate **café**. Otherwise, head back to **Agii Deka** or press on to **Phaistos**.

The ruins of Gortis with the early Christian basilica of Agios Titos

- ✚ 191 E2 ✉ 36km (22mi) southwest of Iraklio
- ☎ 28 92 03 11 44
- 🕐 Daily 8–7 (winter 8:30–3) 🍴 Café (€)
- 🚌 Buses to Phaistos stop at Gortis 🎫 €4

★ Phaistos (Festos)

The Minoan palace at Phaistos is felt by many to be a far more enjoyable site to visit than the better-known Knossos. It stands on a hill overlooking the fertile Mesara Plain, and the fact that it has not been reconstructed allows visitors to view the palace in the best possible way: in the imagination. To see the large central court, the royal apartments, the grand staircase and the nondescript spot where the fabulous Phaistos Disc was found all make for a memorable experience.

The approach to Phaistos is part of its charm, especially if you have already seen Knossos. There are no parking attendants here trying to lure you into their parking lots, just a small car park at the end of a zigzag climb up a little hill. You then walk along the approach to the site to buy a ticket. After entering the site beyond the bookshop, souvenir store and café, you are greeted with a good overall view of the layout.

It is thought that the views were part of Phaistos's original attraction for the Minoans, with the palace built in a way that makes the most of them. Prior to their settlement, it seems others enjoyed the setting, as deposits have been found going back to neolithic and early Minoan periods (3000–2000BC).

Phaistos looks out over the Mesara Plain

Phaistos (Festos)

The first palace here, dated from about 1900BC, is known as the Old Palace and some of its remains can still be seen on the western edge of the site. Destroyed and repaired twice before its ultimate destruction in an earthquake in 1700BC, it was replaced by the New Palace, which remained in use until the end of the Minoan civilisation.

Exploring the Palace

The first open space you come to, the **west court**, is a good place to try to picture the palace as it would have been. Go down into the court and look towards the easily recognisable grand staircase. To the right of this are the remains of the western façade of the palace, built to bask in the glow of the setting sun. To the north of the court is the theatre area, and to the south some large storage pits, used principally for grain.

If you climb the grand staircase you'll see to the right the storerooms within the palace itself, where grain and oil were stored in the type of vast storage jars or *pithoi* that can be seen in almost every museum on Crete. It is not known for sure if the commodities stored at the palace were given to the royal family by way of a tithe, or if the building acted as a secure storage area for everyone to use.

To the east of this you enter the impressive **central court**, a vast open area whose paving dates from 1900 to 1700BC. If you walk to the southern end of this there are good views over the plain, still a source of grain and oil today. It is the largest and most fertile of all the plains on Crete, producing huge crops of olives, citrus and other fruit, and many types of vegetable.

To the north of the central court the area becomes a little confusing, as the remains are on two levels, but beyond

Insider Tip

THE PHAISTOS DISC

Only about 15cm (6in) in diameter, the Phaistos Disc, now in the Archaeological Museum in Iraklio (▶ 54), is one of the most important and intriguing items ever found on Crete. It dates from between 1700 and 1600BC and was uncovered in 1903. Baked in clay, the disc has spirals of pictograms on either side, including flowers, people and animals. No one has ever cracked the code, but the most favoured theory is that it was a religious object of some kind, with the symbols perhaps being the words to a prayer or hymn.

Founded by King Minos

It is believed that the legendary King Minos founded Phaistos, the second most important Minoan palace after Knossos. Earthquakes frequently damaged the original palace and most of the structures that can be seen today are the remains of the New Palace, dating from 1700–1450BC. The complex was destroyed by fire some time around 1450.

The royal apartments surround a small court

❶ **West court:** The west court is an open theatre area on a lower level. Wide stone steps along its supporting wall served as seating for performances and events, it is also likely that ritual bull-leaping events took place here.

❷ **Main entrance:** A unique, monumental staircase leads up to the main entrance which is formed as a propylaeum, separated into two parts by a massive column. The façade with its projections and depressions is typical of Minoan architecture.

❸ **Central court**: The open paved central court was the core of the building and of palace life. It was lined on the east and west sides with alternating columns and rows of pillars.

❹ **King's apartments:** The royal apartments faced north so that the cooler winds blowing from that direction would provide them with some relief from the summer heat.

Phaistos (Festos)

The grand staircase that leads down into the west court

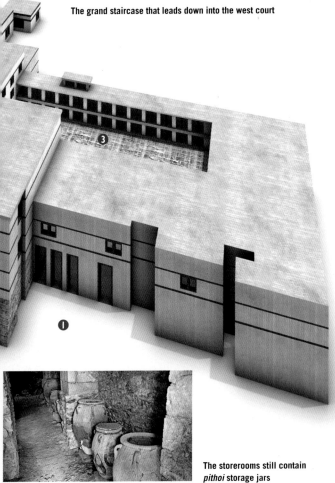

The storerooms still contain *pithoi* storage jars

Central Crete

the small south court, which you may be able to identify, are the **royal apartments**. There are many chambers and antechambers here, one set of rooms belonging to the king and another to the queen.

A well provided water for the palace at Phaistos

If you continue walking past these almost to the edge of the site, you can turn right and see on your right the walls and foundations of a row of small buildings. These were the palace archives, where the **Phaistos Disc** (➤91, panel) was found, a small object that preserves its secrets, just as the palace of Phaistos preserves its own air of mystery and beauty.

TAKING A BREAK

The **on-site café** is the only place to get something to eat for miles around, but it serves plenty of snacks and simple meals and has a lovely dining terrace with views of the countryside.

✚ 191 D2
☎ 28 92 04 23 15
🕐 Daily 8–7:30 (winter 8:30–5) 🍴 Café (€)
🚌 From Iraklio take the Phaistos or Matala bus 🎫 €4

INSIDER INFO

Insider Tip

- As Phaistos is open till late in summer, visit the nearby site of **Agia Triada** (➤ 98) first, which closes earlier.
- Phaistos has a few **benches and shady spots**, making it a pleasant place to relax as well as sightsee.
- If you walk beyond the archives and then turn right, you will reach an open area, the **east court**, in which the remains of a pottery kiln can be seen.
- The leaflet for the site is useful up to a point but if you find the map confusing, buy a more **detailed site guide** in the little bookshop, and make use of those shady trees to do some reading and take in the full story.

At Your Leisure

21 Arolithos

Part of a hotel and purpose-built for tourists, Arolithos may not appeal to everyone. However, if you're yearning to see artisans at work and haven't yet had the chance, this recreation of a traditional village may be what you're looking for. Here you can see weavers, potters and icon painters at work in their ateliers, and learn how *rakí* is made in the agricultural history museum **Insider Tip**

- ✚ 191 F4
- ✉ 10km (6mi) southwest of Iraklio
- ☎ 28 10 82 10 50; www.arolithos.com
- 🕐 Apr–Oct Mon–Sat 8–4; Nov–Mar Mon–Fri 9–5, Sat–Sun 10–6, Oct–Mar
- 🍴 Café (€) 👐 €1.50

22 Tilissos

The remains of this ancient Minoan town sit within the village of the same name, a delightful example of the continuity of life through the ages. This small peaceful spot beneath shady pines is little visited and makes a refreshing change from the larger archaeological sites. **Insider Tip**

It centres on three Minoan villas, which are thought to have been part of a larger community. Tilissos was one of the first Minoan sites to be excavated, prompted by the discovery of three giant bronze cauldrons; these and other finds are now in the Archaeological Museum in Iraklio (➤ 54). The ruins are well preserved, and you can wander among the stone walls and through doorways into small rooms and courtyards. The olive groves and vineyards, where sweet, dark Malmsey wine has been produced since Venetian times, surround the village.

- ✚ 191 E3
- ✉ 14km (9mi) southwest of Iraklio
- ☎ 28 10 83 12 41 🕐 Tue–Sun 8:30–3
- 🚌 Iraklio–Anogia bus stops at Tilissos 👐 €2

23 Agii Deka

Insider are frescoed arches and beautiful woodcarvings, including one of Christ with the martyrs' heads. Two painted icons depict their decapitation, and there is a

The bell tower at Agii Deka

stone block said to have been used for the execution. The New Church, at the west end of the village towards Gortis, is a simple chapel. Below is a crypt, visible from the outside, where you can peer through an iron gate to see six of the martyr's tombs.

➕ 191 E2
✉️ 35km (22mi) southwest of Iraklio
🕐 Daily 🚌 From Iraklio take the Phaistos or Matala bus 🎟️ Free

24 Fodele

This pleasant village, surrounded by orange groves, claims to be the birthplace of El Greco (➤ 24). A memorial plaque to the painter is on display in the shady town square, and across a small bridge spanning the river is the church, which has many copies of El Greco's works.

To see his alleged birthplace, continue along the path (signposted) out of town beside the orchards for about a kilometre. The house is greatly restored and contains a few displays of the painter's life. Opposite the house is the delightful Church of the Panagia. Built in the early 14th century, it incorporates the nave of an earlier 8th-century basilica. The baptismal font beside the church – set in the floor for total immersion – also dates from this period. Partially restored frescoes depict angels, saints and scenes from Christ's life.

Domenikos Theotokopoulos, better known as El Greco

➕ 191 E4
✉️ 25km (16mi) west of Iraklio
☎️ 28 10 52 15 00 (museum)
🕐 Museum and church Tue–Sun 9–3
🚌 Direct bus from Iraklio 🎟️ Free

25 Anogia

The mountain village of Anogia has suffered greatly at the hands of foreign invaders over the years. The Turks destroyed it twice after rebellions in 1821 and 1866, and in August 1944 German troops shot every male in the village and burned every house to the ground in retaliation for the abduction of General Kreipe (➤ 28). Two statues commemorating the freedom fighters stand in the squares in the upper part of town.

Anogia is best known though for its woven goods and embroidery. Brightly coloured textiles drape the streets of the lower town and you may see the local women at work inside their shops.

Behind the café tables in Platia Livadhi notice the odd wooden sculpture of Elefthérios Venizélos (➤ 11). It is the work of the late local artist Alkibiades Skoulas, whose son has opened a museum (open daily 9–7) to display his father's works. Anogia is also renowned as a centre of *lyra* music; many top musicians have come from here.

Insider Tip

🚩 191 E3
✉ 35km (22mi) southwest of Iraklio
🚌 Buses from Iraklio and Rethimnon

26 Oros Psiloritis & Ideon Andron

At 2,456m (8,060ft), Mount Ida is the highest summit on Crete. The locals call it **Psiloritis**, "the high one". Its twin peaks, capped with snow late into spring, are often hidden in cloud, but when the powerful granite bulk is revealed you can understand why it is thought to be Zeus's birthplace (➤ panel).

From Anogia a good paved road winds 22km (14mi) up through the stark, rocky landscape to the **Nida Plateau**. At an altitude of 1,400m (4,593ft) the area is used in the summer as grazing grounds for thousands of sheep and goats. The trip takes about half an hour each way. Birds of prey circle overhead, and you pass round stone shepherds' huts, or *mitata*. Most are now abandoned but were once used as summer dwellings and for making yoghurt and cheese from sheep's milk. The drive is especially pretty in late spring, when the rugged landscape is ablaze with wild flowers.

As you climb higher you may find you are driving through low-lying clouds. Be warned, however, that the road may be closed in winter when it snows.

The road opens out with fine views over the fertile Nida Plateau far below. From here, a 30-minute walk brings you to the **Ideon Andron**. A place of pilgrimage and cult worship since Minoan times, the cave yielded a wealth of artefacts from throughout Greece

BIRTHPLACE OF ZEUS

Mythologists argue over whether the god Zeus was born in the Ideon Cave or the Dikteon Cave (➤ 121). His mother, Rhea, had to bear the child in secrecy because his father, Kronos, Lord of the Titans, had devoured his other offspring, fearing they would someday dethrone him. Guardian warriors, the Kouretes, hid baby Zeus's cries with the clashing of their shields. When Kronos finally tracked Rhea down, she fooled him by giving him a stone wrapped in swaddling clothes to swallow. Zeus grew up with the shepherds on Mount Ida, protected by his grandmother Gaia.

and is mentioned in the works of Greek philosophers Plato and Pythagoras. Experienced hikers can set off from here for the demanding 4-5 hour climb up Psiloritis.

🚩 191 D3 (Ideon Andron), 191 D3 (Psiloritis)
✉ 50km (31mi) southwest of Iraklio
🕐 Cave chambers are currently closed due to excavations 🚌 No public transport

The twin peaks of Mount Ida

Central Crete

27 Mouseio Kritikis Ethnologias

Insider Tip

Located off the beaten track in the village of Voroi, near Phaistos, this excellent folk museum, founded by a local man, is one of the best of its kind on the island. The items are attractively laid out, with information panels in English. Among the ground-floor exhibits are agricultural and domestic items, such as terracotta beehives used since Pharaonic times, furniture, pottery and architecture. Another beautiful collection consists of woven blankets and textiles, and there is an interesting study of door patterns and their relation to status.

The highlight upstairs is a fascinating display of 25 types of baskets, made with different techniques and for different purposes. You can also see musical instruments, numerous weapons and tools, cooking utensils and some wonderful photos of people and festivals.

🕂 191 D2
✉ 3km (2mi) north of Phaistos at Voroi (park on the main street and follow signs to the museum)
☎ 28 92 09 11 12 🕐 Apr–Oct daily 11–5
🍴 On the village square 💰 €3

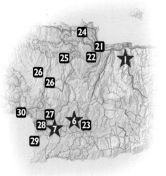

The harvester vase found at Agia Triada

28 Agia Triada

This Minoan site is small-scale after nearby Phaistos, but its intimate nature is the very reason it should be visited. The main ruins consist of a small palace or large royal villa, built in about 1600bc and destroyed, like many other Minoan sites, by a huge fire around 1450bc. Staircases show that the palace had several levels. Fabulous mosaics, jewellery, pottery and other finds have been made here, all now on display at the Archaeological Museum in Iraklio (▶ 54). There is also a cemetery, and the remains of the small town that built up around the palace: a market, shops, houses and workshops. Part of Agia Triada's delight is that no one is quite sure what it was or who lived here, as there are no written references from the Minoan era.

🕂 191 D2
✉ 3km (2mi) northwest of Phaistos
☎ 28 92 0913 60
🕐 Apr–Oct daily 10–4:30,
Nov–Mar Tue–Sun 8:30–3
🚌 Bus to Phaistos 💰 €3
❓ Photography allowed

29 Matala

Matala's days as a hippie haven are long gone, but its caves continue to draw visitors. The caves are man-made, cut into the sandstone cliffs by Romans and early Christians and used as catacombs. In the late 1960s, a commune of hippies moved in and was warmly received by the local population at that time. Some have carved doorways, windows and benches.

The caves form a backdrop to Matala's beach, with taverna balconies overlooking the beach. The picturesque old fishing village on the south side of the bay is particularly appealing. The modern resort part stretches from the beach 2km (1mi) into the valley.

➕ 191 D1
✉ 59km (35mi) southwest of Iraklio ⓒ Caves open Apr–Sep daily 9–5 🚌 Several buses daily from Iraklio 🎫 Caves free

30 Agia Galini

Agia Galini is a pretty resort on the southern coast. Nestled into the surrounding mountains, its whitewashed buildings, dripping with bright bougainvillaea and jasmine, rise up the steep streets from a picturesque harbour. It's now pretty much given over to tourism, and the traffic-free streets in the centre of this former fishing village are lined with shops and restaurants. The sandy beach is a 5-minute walk away from the harbour. There are boat trips from the harbour to Preveli Beach and elsewhere. According to Greek mythology, the rock above the harbour is where Daedalus and Icarus first took flight. There are now two modern sculptures commemorating the myth.

➕ 190 C2 ✉ 45km (28mi) southeast of Rethimnon 🚌 Buses from Rethimnon

Agia Galini rises up from the harbour

Where to…
Stay

Prices
Prices are for a double room per night
€ under €70   €€ €70–€150   €€€ over €150

Fevro Hotel €

This 50-room hotel can be found on the right after the road into Agia Galini descends almost to sea level. Look for where there is a sharp turn left towards the harbour – that's if you can see the hotel name, as the entire building is almost obscured by the most wonderful cascade of colourful bougainvillaea. The clean and simple rooms are a reasonable size, with plain white walls and dark wood furniture. Some have views of the town, and those lower down have "no views but not so many stairs"!

✚ 190 C2 ✉ Agia Galini
☎ 08 32 09 12 75; www.fevro.gr

Palazzo Greco €€

Ideally placed halfway between the town centre and the town beach (on the left of the main road as you first enter Agia Galini), this small boutique hotel is decent and inexpensive, with its own car park opposite. The blue and white front-age matches the 28 bright rooms, those at the back being slightly more expensive because of their balconies and sea views. The buffet breakfast can be taken on the terrace at the back.

✚ 190 C2 ✉ Agia Galini
☎ 28 32 09 11 87; www.palazzogreco.com

Armonia Hotel €

This delightful small hotel, with 27 rooms and pool, is a real find. As you approach Matala on the main road look for it on the left. It is well outside the town so you will need a car, but it makes a great getaway for nature lovers and walkers.

✚ 191 D1 ✉ Matala ☎ 28 92 04 57 35; www.armonia-matala.com May–Oct

Hotel Zafiria €

The main hotel in Matala has 70 typically mid-range rooms – simple and clean – but all have a shower, a radio and a balcony. Some look out towards the sea, others to the hills behind. The hotel has its own bar and restaurant, and owns the mini-market across the street. Although nothing fancy, this makes a good, reasonably priced base.

✚ 191 D1 ✉ Matala ☎ 28 92 04 51 12; www.zafiria-matala.com Apr–Oct

Idi Hotel €

Situated on the edge of the mountain town of Zaros and popular with walkers, the Idi Hotel is an unexpected treat. With its swimming pool and tennis court, bar and Taverna Votomos (➤ 102), it represents excellent value for money. Rooms are in the main hotel block or separate buildings in the beautiful gardens, and are pine-panelled with telephones and air-conditioning. The staff can advise on walking in the Zaros Gorge (➤ 164) and other areas. Activities here include olive-picking, harvesting honey and visits to *raki* distilleries. **Inside Tip**

✚ 191 E2 ✉ Zaros ☎ 28 94 03 13 02; www.idi-hotel.com All year

Where to...
Eat and Drink

Prices
Prices are for a main course for one person, excluding drink
€ under €15   €€ €15–€20   €€€ over €20

Charlie's Place €€
Charlie's Place is a popular spot with great character. Wooden tables are crammed together in one room, spilling into the street. The kitchen is at the back, a tiny place where the owner, Charlie, a Greek-Cypriot, cooks, grills meat, prepares drinks and writes out bills in a whirr of frenetic activity. The menu is small and traditionally Greek, and the meat comes from local farms. One of the busiest places in town, so arrive early or be prepared to wait.
➕ 190 C2 ✉ Agia Galini
☎ 28 32 09 10 65
🕐 Daily 7pm–late

Madame Hortense €€
Climb the flight of wooden stairs and pass a large collection of evocative black and white photos of Cretan characters and scenes to reach a large room with wooden flooring and great open views over the harbour.

There are plenty of Greek and Cretan specialities on the menu. Chicken with peas and olives is one speciality, as is the house version of *kleftiko*: lamb wrapped in filo pastry and baked in the oven. The service includes an aperitif of ouzo served in a beautiful little bottle of coloured glass and a small plate of *mezedes*.
➕ 190 C2
✉ Agia Galini
☎ 28 32 09 12 15
🕐 Daily 6pm–late

O Faros €
This unpretentious little fish taverna, one of the oldest in town, is run by a fishing family serving whatever they catch that day. The tables on the pedestrian street are waited on by the friendly father or his son, who will invite you into the kitchen to choose your fish. They also offer daily cruises to local beaches and islands, including the chance to catch your own fish and have it cooked for you the same evening.
➕ 190 C2 ✉ Agia Galini
☎ 28 32 09 1346
🕐 Daily 6:30pm–late

Insider Tip

Onar €€
Insider is modern and spacious with lots of timber, plus attractive murals and wall hangings. Excellent food and wonderfully friendly service are the hallmarks here, with food grilled over charcoal a speciality. One excellent dish is barracuda fillet with a tomato and garlic sauce.
➕ 190 C2 ✉ Agia Galini
☎ 28 32 09 11 21
🕐 Mar–Nov daily 8am–1am

Potamida €€
Standing right by the beach, the Potamida is one of the biggest restaurants in a row of cafés and tavernas, distinctive with its blue and white décor. It has sunbeds and umbrellas on the beach. The menu offers a huge choice of dishes, particularly salads and pastas, but fresh seafood is the speciality. Indeed,

you might see the chef wading into the sea in the morning with his harpoon gun to catch the fish of the day.

✚ 190 C2 ⊠ Agia Galini
☎ 28 32 09 11 21
⏱ Mar–Oct daily 9am–11:30pm

Corali €€

The lemon paintwork of the Corali stands out on Matala's little square. Here food is served until the last customers leave. You'll have to wait till lunchtime if you want hot dishes though; these include a good range of the usual Greek fare and fresh fish, but there are pizzas too if you fancy a change.

✚ 191 D1 ⊠ Matala
☎ 28 92 04 57 44
⏱ Apr–Oct daily 10am–late

Lions Restaurant €€

Looking right over the beach, Lions has an upper taverna/bar where you can have drinks and snacks, or choose from the full menu in the slightly smarter restaurant downstairs. The chef lived in Australia for 30 years and as a result the menu here is more eclectic than in many Crete restaurants: it's one of the few places on Crete where you'll see Coquilles St Jacques, for example, while another speciality is sole stuffed with crabmeat.

✚ 191 D1 ⊠ Matala
☎ 28 92 04 51 08
⏱ Apr–Oct daily 9am–late

Skala €

To find Skala, go to the very far end of the waterfront to the south and walk through what seems like the last taverna and up some steps; the restaurant is perched on top of the rocks beyond. Family owned, it's a very simple but very popular place, with a great view across the water to the beach. The large open dining terrace with cheerful blue and white walls and doors fills quickly, so arrive early. Fish is the speciality on the menu.

✚ 191 D1 ⊠ Matala ☎ 28 92 04 54 89
⏱ Apr–Oct daily 9am–late

La Strada €€

The cheery blue and white tables on the street contrast with the rustic Italian décor inside, where there is more seating, as well as on the roof terrace. Outside a blackboard lists the day's specials, while the menu has a whole page devoted to pizzas and other Italian dishes, although the wine list is resolutely Greek. La Strada is always busy but the service is brisk.

✚ 191 D1 ⊠ Agia Galini ☎ 28 32 09 10 53
⏱ Daily noon–3, 6–midnight

Taverna Giannis €

This is a real family taverna, found on the right just beyond the small main square. It's as simple as you could get, with a few tables inside and out, serving barrel wine only. You could try one of their specials, such as a Cretan plate of octopus, squid, potatoes and vegetables, or opt for one of the simple Greek dishes. While the choices may be unsurprising they are very well prepared and service friendly.

✚ 191 D1 ⊠ Matala
⏱ Apr–Oct daily noon–late

Votomos Taverna €€

This rural restaurant, situated next to the Idi Hotel (➤ 100) by a stream and small watermill, specialises in trout from the nearby hatchery. The menu also offers other fish and meat dishes, with wine from the barrel or from the short list of Cretan wines. There's both indoor and outdoor seating, as well as a large stage used for occasional live music.

✚ 191 E2 ⊠ Zaros ☎ 28 94 03 13 02
⏱ Mar–Oct daily 11am–midnight;
Nov–Feb Sat–Sun 11am–midnight

Where to…
Shop

You'll find the usual tourist shops and stalls at the entrance to **Fodele**, but for something special try **Atelier Keramos**, _Insider Tip_ the ceramic studio of Manolis Grammatikakis and Paraskevi Laskari-Grammatikaki (tel: 28 10 52 13 62), whose family has been making pottery for four generations. They incorporate new designs into traditional styles to create both useful and decorative pieces. Many designs are available, or you can design your own piece.

Anogia is one of the best-known villages on Crete for textiles, but don't overlook the handicrafts in smaller villages.

At **Tilissos**, for example, right next to the archaeological site, a woman and her daughters have a tiny shop where they sell beautiful and intricate handmade embroidered pieces at very good prices.

Colourful blankets, wall hangings, bags and other pieces made on the loom, or handstitched embroidery or lacework, such as tablecloths or curtains, are items to look for, but be aware that more and more textiles are imported these days. If the stitching on the back is rough and uneven, it's probably hand-done, whereas smooth stitches indicate a factory-sewn item. Another tip is to look for shops where the proprietor herself is working on a piece of embroidery or on a loom. You are welcome to watch, but be prepared for a sales pitch afterwards.

At **Arolithos**, where there is a small row of workshops, you can watch potters, weavers, jewellery-makers, silversmiths, icon painters and other artists create beautiful pieces using time-honoured methods.

Among the many shops in Agia Galini a few stand out. **Labyrinth** (tel: 28 32 09 10 57), in the tiny pedestrianised centre, is where Savas Tsimpouras makes beautiful gold and silver jewellery, as well as rings and necklaces adorned with rose quartz, tourmaline and other precious stones. He also makes replicas of the honey-bee brooch in Iraklio's Archaeological Museum and other Minoan works, and will create pieces to order.

A few doors away, next to the Blue Bar, is **Eli**, an artist who creates outstanding pottery in her workshop at the back of the shop. Her work, from female figures to mobiles to beautifully shaped vases, is unique.

You will also find lots of olive-wood souvenirs in Agia Galini. Try **Wood Shop Maria** in the centre for a good selection of handmade items.

Le Shop, just round the corner from La Strada restaurant (► 102), sells a nice range of quality leather items, silver jewellery and books and newspapers in several languages, including novels and books about Crete.

Matala has a covered market area lined with souvenir stalls, but nothing outstanding is to be found here.

The nicest shop is **Natura Minoika**, on the main street, which sells natural Cretan products such as herbed olive oils, soaps and sponges, and popular art made from olive wood.

Where to...
Go Out

Agia Galini is the hotspot for nightlife in central Crete.

Young Cretans from the Mesara area meet at the **Alibi Bar** by the waterfront to stop for a drink.

Paradiso (Paradise Bar), a roof-garden bar up the steps from the waterfront, is a favourite for dancing and has a happy hour from 10pm to midnight.

Also good for dancing are **Cactus, Juke Box** and **Escape**, all near each other by the harbour. Here the music hots up after 11 pm.

Smaller, atmospheric spots for socialising over good music include **Blue Bar**, opposite Faros taverna, and **Jazz n'Jazz** at the top end of the central pedestrianised area.

In **Matala**, on the road heading south parallel to the beach, the place to be is the famous **Rock Bar**, and it is not unusual to find young people from Iraklio who have come for the evening. Despite the name, a range of music is played.

Marinero next door is another option. For a Latin beat and world music over cocktails, try **Kantari** on the main square.

Club opening hours vary widely, with some (particularly those that are also cafés) being open all day, others opening early evening and some not till 10pm or so. Clubs and discos seldom open before 10pm or 11pm and don't really get going till midnight. During high season in summer, clubs and discos are open nightly, but in low season they are often open only on weekends.

If it's Greek music you're after, there are "Greek nights" including live music and dancing at many tavernas on weekends in summer. Travel agencies in **Agia Galini** can also book Greek nights for you.

A host of **water sports** is available at Agia Galini, including water-skiing, paragliding, jet skis, banana boats and paddleboats.

Tour operators in town can book **boat trips** to more remote beaches, such as Agios Georgios and Agios Pavlos, and to the sandy beaches of Paximadia Island, 12km (7mi) offshore. There are trips to the Samaria and Imbros gorges (► 146 and 153), or Preveli Beach and Monastery (► 152).

The **Argonaut**, operated by the owners of the O Faros (► 101), will take you on cruises, fishing trips or excursions to Gavdos Island and local beaches.

For boat trips from Matala to nearby Red Beach and elsewhere, check with a local travel agent. Some of Matala's beaches are spawning grounds for sea turtles, an endangered species.

The **Melanouri Horse Farm** (tel: 2892045040; www.melanouri.com) is signposted from the village of Pitsidia, northeast of Matala. Here the riding centre caters for all ages, including children, and offers rides along Kommos Beach and full-moon rides – a chance to explore the beautiful and fertile Mesara Plain.

Eastern Crete

 **Little Treats**

Making optimal use of space

At **Mary's Kitchen** in Sitia (► 118; Odos
A. Papandreou 4) some of the tables even
spill out on to the verge of the road.

Waterfront art

On the seaside promenade at Limenas
Chersonisou (► 121) you can admire a
Roman fountain with mosaics of fishing scenes.

Overlooking Agios

The Alexandros roof top bar (Odos Kondilaki 1)
offers beautiful **night-time views** over the lake
at Agios Nikolaos (► 112).

Getting Your Bearings

Northeastern Crete has seen some of the densest tourism development on the island, particularly in the north between Iraklio and Kolpos Mirampellou (Gulf of Mirabello), where bustling resorts have gobbled up the coastal landscape. Beyond the bay, however, the far eastern region holds some of the most stunning scenery on the island, from rugged mountains to an unexpected palm beach.

Crete's main centre of package tourism lies east of the capital, stretching along the north coast to Malia. Here a string of burgeoning resorts have all but usurped the old villages with cheek-by-jowl hotels, apartments, restaurants, bars, travel agencies and souvenir shops. Agios Nikolaos, set prettily around a little lake, is another bustling centre. Amid this hedonistic coastal strip, the ancient palace of Malia and the Minoan town of Gournia anchor this changing landscape to the past.

A short drive inland takes you into another world. The provincial town of Neapoli is a gateway to timeless farming villages of the Lasithiou Plateau. High in the Dikti Mountains is the birthplace of the Greek god Zeus. At Kritsa, the fresco-covered Church of Panagia Kera is an artistic jewel, while the nearby site of Lato offers archaeological ruins from Greek antiquity.

The famous palm beach of Vaï

A stunning coastal drive, not to be missed, brings you further east to Sitia, with its attractive waterfront and relaxed pace. From here you can strike out across a starkly beautiful mountainous landscape to reach Moni Toplou, the palm-fringed Vaï Beach and the Minoan palace at Zakros.

Ierapetra, Europe's southernmost town, is the largest on the south coast, with more fine beaches at small resorts to either side.

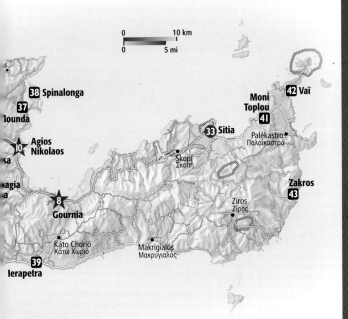

Top 10

Don't Miss

At Your Leisure

Five Perfect Days

If you're not quite sure where to begin your travels, this itinerary recommends a practical and enjoyable five-day tour of eastern Crete, taking in some of the best places to see. For more information see the main entries (➤ 110–120).

Day One

Morning

Get an early start from **34 Malia** (➤ 121) or **36 Neapoli** (➤ 122). Follow the drive around the **Lasithiou Plateau** (➤ 168) and visit the **35 Dikteon Andron** (➤ 121). Then take some time for a little walk through the fields on the plain before making your way to one of villages for a bite to eat in one of the modest tavernas or *kafeníon*.

Afternoon

Aim to reach **31 Malia Palati** (➤ 114) by 2pm to explore the ancient ruins, then hit the beach for a swim.

Evening

Spend the evening either in Malia's old town, in the quaint village of Koutouloufari – above Limenas Chersonisou – or in "Old" Chersonisos, a picturesque village a little further inland.

Day Two

Morning

Visit **32 Kritsa** and **Panagia Kera** (➤ 116) early to beat the crowds. Have lunch by the beach at the **Barko** restaurant (➤ 129) in Agios Nikolaos.

Afternoon

Drive to **37 Elounda** (photo above, ➤ 122) and take the boat trip to **38 Spinalonga Island** (➤ 123).

Evening

Stay in Elounda and dine by the waterfront at the **Ferryman's Taverna** (➤ 129) or **Vritomartes** (➤ 130).

Day Three

Morning

Drive to ⭐ **Agios Nikolaos** (➤ 112), take a stroll around the lake before visiting the local museums and the cathedral of Agia Triada, then stop for lunch in the courtyard of the **Pelagos** restaurant (➤ 129).

Afternoon/Evening

Explore the Minoan ruins at
☆ **Gournia** (➤ 110) then make the
short drive south across the isthmus
to **39 Ierapetra** (photo right, ➤ 123).
From here, continue west to **40 Mirtos**
(➤ 124) for a relaxing drink beside
the sea. Stay the night here and have
dinner at **Taverna Akti** (➤ 130).

Day Four

Morning

Return via Ierapetra to the north
coast and take the spectacular cliff
road that runs along the coast to
33 Sitia (➤ 118).

Afternoon

Have lunch at one of Sitia's waterfront tavernas, but tear yourself away by
2pm to visit the **Archaeological Museum** (➤ 119). Afterwards, sun yourself
on the town beach.

Evening

Visit the **Folk Museum** (➤ 119) and return to the waterfront for dinner at
The Cretan House (➤ 130).

Day Five

Morning

Get an early start from Sitia for the winding drive to **43 Zakros Palati**
(➤ 125). Have lunch at **Kato Zakros Bay Restaurant** (➤ 130).

Afternoon

On the return through Palékastro continue north for a swim at the beach
at **42 Vaï** (➤ 125). Leave by 4:30pm to reach **41 Moni Toplou** (➤ 124),
which is open until 6pm.

Evening

Return to Sitia for dinner at **The Balcony** (➤ 130).

8 Gournia

Crete's great Minoan palaces tend to get all the glory, overshadowing the other surviving remnants from the civilisation, which was widespread, particularly in the east. Gournia is the largest town yet uncovered and its superbly preserved ruins give a fascinating insight into everyday life in Minoan times. This was a real work-a-day town, where tradesmen such as potters, bronzesmiths and carpenters went about their daily affairs.

Though Gournia was settled in early Minoan times, the ruins you see today date from around 1500BC, when the town was at its peak. It flourished because of its splendid position above Kolpos Mirampellou (Gulf of Mirabello), making it commercially as well as strategically important. It had its own harbour and traded with Ierapetra on the south coast via an overland route across the isthmus (at 12km/7mi the narrowest point on the island), thus avoiding the dangerous sea journey round the eastern shores.

Destroyed in the cataclysm of 1450BC (➤ 17), Gournia rose from its ashes during Mycenaean times but was finally abandoned in 1200BC. A young American archaeologist,

A maze of streets and steps at Gournia

Harriet Boyd Hawes (1871–1945), excavated it around the same time that Phaistos and Knossos were being excavated (1901).

Exploring Gournia

On entering the site, you immediately notice how well preserved it is. The foundations of hundreds of houses, up to a metre or more high, spread up the hillside; these were the basements, used as store-rooms or workshops, with living areas in the upper storeys that have long since vanished. Tools found in some of these buildings identified various tradesmen and craftsmen, farmers and fishermen, providing great insight into domestic life in Minoan times. Cobbled streets, wide enough for pack animals but not wheeled carts, wound through the town, dividing it into seven neighbourhoods. Even today, mountain villages on Crete follow this layout.

You can take the path straight ahead up the stone steps, or turn left along what was formerly a main street, still with its original paving. Both lead to the town centre at the top of the hill. At its heart was the palace, smaller than but similar in style to Knossos and Malia. It was probably the seat of the local governor.

To the south, L-shaped stairs lead to a large court-yard that was the agora, or market-place. The large stone slab next to the stairs may have been a sacrificial altar (or simply a butcher's block). To the north was the sanctuary, where a shrine with snake-goddess figures and other cult objects was found.

As you survey the site from the top of the acropolis remember that Gournia was four times larger than what you see today. Imagine it stretching northward all the way to the sea, as it did in antiquity.

TAKING A BREAK

There are **no refreshments** at Gournia, so bring your own water and snacks.

➕ 193 E3 ☎ 28 42 09 30 28 🕐 Tue–Sun 8–4 🚌 Buses from Agios Nikolaos to Sitia and Ierapetra can drop you near the site 💶 €2

INSIDER INFO

- Save for a couple of small trees, **there is no shade**. Wear sunblock, hat and sun-glasses for protection.
- Gournia is **delightful in springtime** when colourful wild flowers blossom amid the stones.
- The **turning off the National Highway** (New Road) is easy to miss. Driving east, a few kilometres beyond Istro start to look for the sign for Gournia, just beyond, on a sudden right turn on to a gravel road.

Insider Tip

⭐ 10 Agios Nikolaos

The town of Agios Nikolaos with its twin harbours is one of the most attractive on Crete. Its popularity means that it is also one of the busiest, but if you don't mind the crowds you can enjoy its restaurants and nightlife. It also has an excellent archaeological museum with fine Minoan treasures.

Life centres round the two harbours, although the inner one is actually a tiny lake, linked to the main harbour by a narrow channel. Lake Voulismeni is also known as the Bottomless Lake, a slight exaggeration but it does have very steep sides and a middle depth of some 64m (210ft). Bars, cafés, restaurants and souvenir shops line the lake and harbour, and the area buzzes from morning till night.

View of Agios Nikolaos

The town has always been a port, in ancient times for the inland city of Lato (▶ 116), and later for the Venetians. They named the town after a 10th-century church dedicated to St Nicholas, and they also dubbed the gulf on which it stands Mirabello, or Beautiful View.

The small **Folklore Museum**, by the bridge between the lake and the main harbour, has exhibits that represent the old lifestyle of rural Crete. Two shop-lined main streets – one of which is pedestrianised – lead from the main harbour uphill to the town square with the cathedral of **Agia Triada**. The interior is of the church is entirely decorated with new frescoes done in the traditional Byzantine style.

Insider Tip

Archaeological Museum

It's a steep climb, but one worth making, up to the town's excellent Archaeological Museum. Take the rooms, arranged around a small interior courtyard, in a clockwise direction.

After various displays of unusual objects, such as the earliest known fish-hooks on Crete and the longest early-Minoan dagger, you come to the museum's star attraction: the **Goddess of Mirtos**. This exquisite piece, dating from around 2500BC, depicts an unusual bell-shaped figure holding a jug in her stick-like arms. It was probably used for a fertility ritual. Further on are ceramics, coins, votive figures and many unique objects, such as a late Minoan burial *pithos* from Krya with the skeleton inside. In Room IX, a local Roman 1st century tomb was found to contain the skull of an athlete crowned with a golden laurel and a silver coin resting in his jaw – to pay the ferryman to the Underworld.

The cathedral of Agia Triada

TAKING A BREAK

Several places to eat fringe the **harbour and the lake**, but one of the established favourites for visitors and locals is **Barko** (➤ 129), open from breakfast till late.

Insider Tip

✚ 193 E3

Archaeological Museum
✉ Palaiologou 68 ☎ 28 41 02 49 43
🕑 Expected to reopen 2015/16
🅿 Parking in streets and car park near by
💶 Most likely €4

Folklore Museum
✉ Palaiologou 2 ☎ 28 41 02 50 93
🕑 Tue–Sun 10–2 🅿 Parking further on around the waterfront 💶 €3

Agia Triada
✉ Platia El Venizelou
🕑 Daily 7–noon and 4–7:30
💶 Free, donations welcome

INSIDER INFO

- Traffic is bad, so **avoid driving into the centre** if you can. You can park in the streets on the hill where the Archaeological Museum stands, or at the marina.
- The **Goddess of Mirtos** in the Archaeological Museum is a must see.
- The **Folklore Museum** by the channel between the lakes is not bad, but could be skipped if time is short.

③① Malia Palati

Set on a flat plain along the northern coast, the island's third largest Minoan palace may lack the grandeur of Phaistos or Knossos, but the beautiful reddish hues of its substantial stone walls give it an evocative beauty of its own. It is also less crowded and easier to fathom than its bigger sisters, making for an enjoyable place to wander back in time.

First built around 1900BC, Malia Palace was destroyed by earthquakes and rebuilt around 1650BC, after which it stood for another 200 years. The ruins date from the latter period. After its discovery in 1915 excavations were taken over by the French Archaeological School in Athens. These are still continuing, and the remains of a substantial town are being unearthed to the north and west of the main site. Some areas that were built of mud brick have been placed under canopies to prevent them being eroded by rain and wind.

Exploring the Ruins

The entrance to the palace is through the west court. You can weave your way through the thick stone walls of the west magazines (storerooms). Alternatively, turn right and head to the southwest corner where there are eight round granary pits. Follow the south side to a wide stone-paved passage that leads into the central court, a huge space measuring 48m by 22m (157ft by 72ft).

The **west wing** held the most important sections of the palace, including the loggia, an elevated room looking on to the court, reached by the grand staircase alongside. Below this a hall leads into the pillar crypt, a place of religious ritual. In the court's southwest corner is another large staircase, and beside this is Malia's famous *kernos*. This circular slab of limestone with 34 depressions set around a central hollow is thought to have been a kind of altar in which seed or grain offerings were placed. It may also have been a gaming board.

One of Malia's more curious features is the large number of storage areas throughout the palace. The entire **east wing** was given over to more magazines used for storing liquids in giant *pithoi* (storage jars) placed in sunken pits, complete

INSIDER INFO

Insider Tip

The palace is **3km (2mi) beyond Malia village**, signposted off the New Road.

- For the best **photographs**, visit in the late afternoon when the light brings out the warm colours of the red stone.
- The **museum is very small** with only a site model and some photos and diagrams on the wall.

The circular slab is thought to have been a sacrificial stone

with drainage channels for spillage. On the **north side** is the hypostyle, or pillared hall, and north court. To the west of this were the royal apartments. Two magnificent giant *pithoi* stand guard along the palace's northern edge. Malia yielded some outstanding artefacts, now in the Archaeologial Museum in Iraklio (➤ 54). The famous honeybee pendant was discovered at the grave complex called Chryssolakos (pit of gold), to the northeast of the palace.

TAKING A BREAK

You can buy **drinks and snacks** from a van in the car park, but you'll have to return to **Malia town** for more substantial refreshment.

✚ 192 C4
☎ 28 97 03 15 97 🕐 Tue–Sun 8:30–3
🚌 Buses stop at the National Highway 🎟 €4

㉜ Kritsa & Panagia Kera

The tiny Byzantine Church of Panagia Kera is one of the most famous on Crete, renowned for the 14th- and 15th-century frescoes that cover almost every inch of its interior walls with vivid religious scenes. It stands just outside the traditional village of Kritsa, as does the archaeological site of Lato, and a visit combining all three makes for a fascinating and contrasting couple of hours.

Kritsa

Said to be the largest village in the region, Kritsa sits in the low hills about 10km (6mi) inland from the busy resort of Agios Nikolaos. It can be very crowded when coach parties descend and hundreds of people wander the steep streets searching for the best of the local handicrafts. Weavings, embroidery, lace and leatherware are all here in abundance, and with better prices than you will pay in shops in the resort towns on the coast. When the visitors depart, Kritsa reverts to being an ordinary Cretan village, and an attractive one, too, with its backdrop of mountains and views in places down to the coast.

Insider Tip

Walking through history at Lato

Lato

Signposted from Kritsa, 3km (2mi) north, is the site of ancient Lato. It is well worth visiting both for the drive along the zigzagging valley road up to the site and the magnificent views over the valley when you get there. Lato is one of Crete's lesser-known sites, with comparably fewer visitors, despite being the most important archaeological site from the first millennium BC.

Insider Tip

It dates from the Dorian period, which followed the Minoan and Mycenaean eras, when the Dorian people, originally from northern Greece, ruled Crete and much of the mainland from about 1100BC

until the arrival of the Romans in 69BC. Lato was an important city, as can be seen by the extent of the remains along the hillside. Excavations did not begin until 1957 and much work still needs to be done. Areas uncovered so far include the agora, or market-place, steps that were part of a theatre, the foundations of shops and artisans' workshops and what was probably the original gate to the old city. The best part of the experience is simply being there, however, as the site has a unique charm.

Fresco in the
Panagia Kera

Panagia Kera

Insider Tip

The highlight of eastern Crete is the delightful Church of Panagia Kera, a little domed beige building with just three tiny aisles. It is reached by a path from the main road. With the exception of the stone floors, the church interior is covered in frescoes. Some of the colours are a little dulled with time, but the details are as clear and as beautiful as when they were first painted during the 14th and 15th centuries. The sheer volume of images, including icons of the saints, biblical scenes and graphic depictions of the punishments that sinners can expect in Hell, is overwhelming.

TAKING A BREAK

There are several cafés and tavernas in **Kritsa**. The **Paradise Snack Bar** opposite Panagia Kera is open all day for everything from coffee to meals.

Lato
➕ 193 E3 ✉ Kritsa
🕐 Apr–Oct 8–3 🎟 €2

Panagia Kera
➕ 193 E3 ✉ Kritsa 🕐 Apr–Oct 8:30–3
🚌 Buses to Kritsa from Agios Nikolaos 🎟 €4

INSIDER INFO

- Early morning and late afternoon are the **quietest times to visit** Kritsa.
- In the central aisle of Panagia Kera, on the right-hand side near the door, is a delightful and moving portrait of the *Virgin and Child*; the two figures are exchanging the most loving of looks.
- The **Church of Panagia Kera** is on the right as you approach Kritsa from Agios Nikolaos, but the signs are small. Easier to spot is the Paradise Snack Bar, on the left-hand side of the road. The ticket office is opposite.

㉝ Sitia

If for no other reason, visit Sitia for the magnificent drive that takes you there through some of the finest scenery on Crete. Beyond Agios Nikolaos the National Highway becomes a high cliff road that winds up and down the mountainsides with tantalising glimpses of the sea. Once in Sitia, you'll be delighted by its atmosphere. Set around a beautiful bay, it's more laid-back town than tourist resort and makes an excellent base from which to explore the attractions of the far eastern end of the island.

Crete's fifth largest town sits on the western side of the pretty Bay of Sitia, its sun-bleached houses climbing up the hillside above the waterfront. A wide promenade curves along the harbour, shaded by squat palms and backed by a ring of pleasant tavernas that provide the perfect spot to chill out and watch the colourful fishing boats bobbing on the water. East of the marina, just beyond the tourist office, is the sandy town beach. Although tourism is growing, locals outnumber tourists here.

Insider Tip

There is much history here. Remains of a substantial Minoan settlement were discovered in the southern suburb of Petras, and more Minoan villas and peak sanctuaries were found in this region of Crete than anywhere else. West of the harbour towards the ferry port are the remains of Roman fish tanks. On the eastern outskirts of town

Sitia's atmospheric harbour

EROTOKRITOS

Vitsentzos Kornáros, author of the epic poem *Erotókritos*, was born in Sitia in the 17th century. Standing on the waterfront by the tourist office is a monument to him, with scenes from his work, which is still sung today (▶ 19).

the ruins of Hellenistic Sitia are under excavation. Earthquakes destroyed the town's Venetian-era buildings, save for the fortress that stands out on the hilltop. It is now used as an open-air theatre, particularly during the town's cultural festival, the **Kornaria**, held in July and August (▶ 132).

Insider Tip

Archaeology Museum

This small but excellent museum contains many treasures from eastern Crete dating from neolithic to Roman times. The first section contains finds from various sites in Minoan Sitia. More than 80 excavated sites indicate the density of settlement in this region. Many beautiful pieces of pottery were discovered in cemeteries and their decoration is outstanding both in quality and preservation. In case 7 an exquisite figure of a bull comes from the cemetery at Mochlos. Crete's best-preserved hieroglyphic archive was discovered at Petras and there are examples in case 27.

Next come exhibits from the Zakros Palati (▶ 125), which yielded many unusual finds. The decoration on the large *pithoi* (storage jars) is superb. There are rare fragments of Linear A tablets, remarkably well preserved due to a cataclysmic fire that acted like a kiln and baked the clay. Another case holds beautiful rounded pitchers,

three-legged pots, tiny vases and curious kitchen utensils, including a terracotta grill.

Post-Minoan-era finds complete the collection. Case 22 holds odd votive objects from an archaic sanctuary: the clay Egyptian-style heads were inserted into phial-shaped bodies, and may have been associated with fertility rites. In the last room a water tank contains a mass of vases compacted in a Roman shipwreck.

Folk Museum

Sitia also has a charming little folk museum, set in a former upper-class house. There are displays of agricultural tools, kitchen implements and a century-old

Eastern Crete

loom, plus fine examples of traditional bedspreads, embroidery and other handiwork. Be sure to go upstairs to see the decorative 1890 bridal bed with silk canopy and coverings.

On the Outskirts

Sitia is one of Crete's best wine producing regions and a **wine co-operative** on the main road into town gives wine tours in summer. This includes a video on the wine-making process, a look around the museum and a tasting of local wines and olive oil, both of which are for sale.

About 2km (1mi) along the beach road, heading east towards Vaï, a signed track on the left marked "Archaeological Site" leads to the Hellenistic site of **Tripitos**, which dates from the 3rd century BC. Park beside the farm building and walk up to the fenced site, which you can enter. The site is still under excavation, but the foundations of many buildings, rooms and streets are visible, and there's a grand view over the sea.

View over the Bay of Sitia

TAKING A BREAK

The attractive cafés and tavernas that line the **western shore** of the Bay of Sitia provide the perfect spot to relax.

Insider Tip

➕ 194 B4

Archaeology Museum
✉ Odos Eleftherias Venizelou, opposite the bus station
☎ 28 43 02 39 17
🕐 Tue–Sun 8:30–3
💰 €2

Folk Museum
✉ Kapetan Sifi 26
☎ 28 43 02 28 61
🕐 Mon–Sat 9:30–1:30 💰 €2

Wine Co-operative
✉ Missonos 74 ☎ 28 43 02 99 91
🕐 Mon–Fri 8:30–2:30
💰 Free

INSIDER INFO

- Sitia's **waterfront** is so pleasant and relaxing that you may find yourself spending an extra day in the town.
- The **ruins of the Roman fish tanks** are largely submerged and almost impossible to make out.

At Your Leisure

34 North Coast Resorts

Limenas Chersonisou

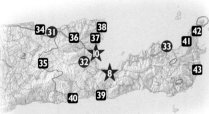

(✚ 192 C4) is the biggest and brashest of the northeast coast resorts. The younger generation and couples are more likely to feel comfortable here; it is not as suitable for families or senior citizens. The main road, 2km (1mi) long, and parallel beach road are packed solid with bars, shops and services, joined by narrow side streets crammed with hotels. But where's the beach? The narrow patches of sand are largely hidden among the hotels and the rocky coastline; the main beach is on the western side of the village. Inland is the picturesque village of "Old" **Chersonisos**, with its quaint squares lined with tavernas.

A few kilometres east is **Malia** (✚ 192 C4), the north coast's other famous party resort. It's just as busy and noisy but mildly more attractive. The sandy beaches, about a kilometre from the main road, can get crowded – those to the east are quieter. The ancient Minoan ruins of Malia Palace (➤ 114) are the main tourist attraction. The old village is uphill on the opposite side of the main road, with some good traditional tavernas along its winding streets and in its pretty square.

In between the two is **Stalida** (✚ 192 C4), or **Stalis**, a burgeoning, tightly packed resort with a sandy beach and quieter nightlife. West of Chersonisos you'll find the smaller resorts of **Kokkini Chani** (✚ 192 B4) and **Kato Gouves** (✚ 192 B4).

35 Dikteon Andron

Located high in the Dikti Mountains above the village of Psichró, this is the most famous and impressive cave on Crete. In mythology it is said to be the birthplace of the god Zeus (➤ 97), and its importance as a cult centre since Minoan times was confirmed by the discovery of a huge number of votive offerings. It remained a place of religious ritual for the Dorian Greeks long after the Minoans' demise.

The 🚹 cave entrance is reached either on foot or by donkey ride (in summer). The 65m (213ft) descent into the depths of the cave has been made easier, if less mysterious, by concrete steps and lighting. The path circles around the bottom, alongside a dark pool, with views of the great stalactites and stalagmites. It takes a little

SOUTH COAST BEACHES

There are numerous sandy bays along Crete's southeast coast, as well as two resorts with very long sand and pebble beaches: **Ierapetra** and 🚹 **Makrigialos-Analipsis**. The hotels in this region are usually pleasantly small and there are also plenty of private apartments and houses for rent. It is also a good place in which to spend the winter.

Dikteon Andron's stalactites and stalagmites

imagination to pick out such features as the "nipples" where the baby god suckled, but with the cave's mouth a mere slit of light far above, you can sense the mystical wonder it held for the ancient Cretans. This is especially true if you beat the crowds by visiting early morning or late afternoon.

✚ 192 C3 ⏱ May–Oct 10–6:30
🍴 Café (€€)
🎟 €4; additional parking fee

36 Neapoli

Tourists largely overlook this market town, but it has much local charm. The roads end at the main square next to the large, modern church. On the south side of the square a small **folklore museum** has local artefacts recalling the traditional way of life. Opposite the war memorial, the café **I Driros** is the place to sample the local speciality – a sweet, milky drink called *soumádha*, made from pressed almonds. It's also a pleasant spot from which to observe the passing scene.

Neapoli makes a good base for exploring the Lasithiou Plateau (▶ 168). Odos Ethnikis Antistasis leads from the square to the town's only hotel, the Neapolis (▶ 128).

✚ 193 D4
🚌 Buses from Agios Nikolaos and Malia

37 Elounda

Situated about 7km (4mi) north of Agios Nikolaos, on the western shores of the Gulf of Mirabello, Elounda is believed to be the place with the most luxury hotels in Crete. The long main road through town leads to a large square set around the harbour, which, lined with cafés and restaurants, is the focal point of activity. Boat trips to Spinalonga Island leave regularly from here. Just beyond the parking area is the sandy town beach.

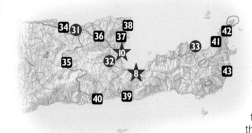

On the southern edge of town – reached by a small road along the shore that passes Venetian salt pans – is a causeway. It runs above a submerged isthmus that once connected the mainland to Spinalonga Peninsula. From here, when the waters are calm, you can see a few remains of the sunken city of **Olous**. Behind the taverna on the causeway a fenced area protects the black and white mosaic floor of a 4th-century church. There are good beaches and birding on the peninsula.

➕ 193 E4 🚌 Bus from Agios Nikolaos

🔢38 Spinalonga

A short boat ride from Elounda brings you to the eeriest place on Crete, tiny Spinalonga Island, commanding the entrance to the bay. The Venetians built a 🏰 fortress here in 1579 to defend the gulf and it remained one of the island's most formidable strongholds long after the Turkish invasion, only handed over by treaty in 1715. Turkish settlers built homes here and refused to leave after Greece won independence. The government persuaded them to go by designating Spinalonga a

Spinalonga Island's Venetian fortress

leper colony in 1903. It was the last of its kind in Europe, and existed until it was evacuated in 1957.

The approach to the island is stunning, with the reflections of the round keep of the fortress and its walls gleaming in the bay. Sometimes, guides meet you on shore to tell the sad tale of life on the "island of the living dead", as it was locally known. There are wonderful views from the ramparts.

➕ 193 E4 🕐 Boats daily in season, every 30 minutes 9:30–4:30
🎫 Boat trip: €10, entrance: €2

🔢39 Ierapetra

With Africa just 300km (186mi) away, Ierapetra is Europe's southernmost city. Though it gets the most sunshine, too, its prosperity comes not from tourism but from the farmers who grow year-round crops of tomatoes and peppers in masses of plastic greenhouses along this coast.

You can take a pleasant stroll (1,2km/0,8mi) along the waterfront that runs from the distinctive Hotel Petra Mare to the small Venetian fort. Opposite the fort is the 14th-century Afentis Christos church bell tower.

The waterfront is lined with countless cafés and restaurants;

Eastern Crete

In the centre of Ierapetra

the eastern section is pedestrianised while a reasonable beach flanks the western section.

Some characterful houses still stand in the winding lanes of the old Turkish quarter, behind the waterfront. Seek out the small square with an ornate Ottoman fountain and a restored Turkish mosque.

The small **Archaeology Museum** has two particular treasures: a 2nd-century statue of Demeter, goddess of fertility, holding an ear of corn; and a Minoan *larnax*, or lidded clay coffin, with superb decoration depicting a wild goat hunt and other figures.

A long, sandy beach stretches west of town, or take a boat trip to the more appealing 👫 beaches of **Chrisi Island**, 12km (7mi) offshore.

✚ 193 E2 Archaeology Museum
☎ 28 42 02 87 21 🕐 Tue–Sun 8–3 🖐 €2

🔟 Mirtos

The appeal of this charming south coast village far outweighs its small size. There are no sights, save a two-room local museum, and its long grey sand beach is not out-

standing, but it's the sort of place where people drop in for a day and end up staying for months. A long sandy beach begins just west of the village, at the end of the short (200m/656ft) waterfront where the whole village gathers in the evening.

A beach on Chrisi Island

✚ 193 D2 🚌 Bus from Ierapetra

🔟 Moni Toplou

Alone on a small windy hilltop, Moni Toplou looks more like a fortress than a monastery. In reality, it was. Its name means "cannon" in Turkish, and artillery was installed here in Venetian times after it was sacked by pirates in 1498. Thus began its long history as a centre of resistance.

Toplou owns much of the surrounding land and is said to be one of the richest monasteries in Greece. Its grounds and buildings have been greatly restored. Outside the entrance is an old stone windmill; look inside to see how the huge wooden millstones were turned by the sails to grind flour.

Inside the walls, the pretty cobbled courtyard – bright with flowers and greenery – is surrounded by the monks' cells and the bell tower. The church holds the monastery's great treasure: an 18th-century icon by Ioánnis Kornáros entitled *Lord, Thou Art Great*. It comprises 61 intricate biblical scenes, each illustrating a line from this Greek Orthodox prayer, and is considered a masterpiece of Cretan art. More icons can be seen in the museum and one room highlights the monastery's role in the battle for Cretan independence and during World War II.

🚩 194 C4 ☎ 28 43 06 12 26
🕐 Daily 9–1, 2–6
🍴 Café (€) at the entrance to the monastery
💶 €3

42 Vaï

Although the crowds that flock to Crete's famous palm beach can mar the idyllic environment they've come to see, it's still worth a visit especially off-season when you'll be alone. For the most scenic approach, take the road that passes Moni Toplou and as you descend through the stark landscape remi-

Looking down at Paralia Vaï

niscent of North Africa, a **forest of date palms** suddenly rises up oasis-like before you. *Phoenix theophrasti* is unique to eastern Crete, the last of a palm species that was once widespread in the southeast Aegean. Some say the grove grew from date stones spat out by Egyptian soldiers who camped here, others that the date-eaters were pirates. The grove covers 20 hectares (50 acres) in a narrow valley stretching to the beach. Tour buses call in here during summer, when the **wide sandy beach** is generally packed for much of the day. It quietens down around 4pm, so come early or late in the day to appreciate its beauty.

🚩 194 C4
🍴 Restaurant (€) on the beach
🚌 Buses from Sitia and Makrygialos
🅿 Pay-parking

43 Zakros Palati

If you make time to visit the fourth of Crete's great Minoan palaces, at the remote eastern reaches of the island, you'll be well rewarded. From Sitia the winding road takes you across a beautiful high plateau ringed by mountains.

Eastern Crete

Allow an hour (minimum) to get to the ancient site, which lies 8km (5mi) beyond Ano Zakros (the upper town) at sea-level Kato Zakros. Here a few pleasant tavernas face an idyllic pebble beach.

Built around 1900BC, Zakros had a fine harbour and was the island's main naval base, flourishing on trade with Egypt and the Middle East. Like the other great Minoan palaces, it too was destroyed by catastrophic events around 1450BC.

However, because the site was so isolated it had never been looted and when it was excavated in the 1960s more than 10,000 artefacts were found, many of them unique. Magnificent ivory, bronze and stoneware, including elaborate vases and chalices, are now in the museums at Iraklio and Sitia.

The dig yielded another remarkable find: in a ritual well filled with spring water the archaeologists discovered a votive cup of olives some 3,000 years old. Before the olives could disintegrate, the crew bravely tasted them – and found them as delicious as if they had just been picked.

Though Zakros is similar in design to the other palaces, it is far more peaceful and atmospheric. To the west of the central court and banquet hall is the central shrine, an archive where hundreds of Linear A tablets were stored, and the treasury where the famous rock crystal *rhyton* (➤ 58) was found.

The large round cistern, like the other wells, is full of terrapins. Beyond this, under a canopy, is a bathroom where visitors might have washed before entering the court. You can see the basins and traces of red fresco.

Large stone steps lead to the exit, which was the original entrance to the palace from the harbour road. Rising up the hillside are the ruins of the Upper Town, which afford great views over the entire site.

🗺 194 C3
☎ 28 43 06 12 04
🕐 May–Oct daily 8–8, Nov–April Tue–Sun 8:30–3
🚌 Bus from Sitia 💶 €3

Surveying the Palace from Ano Zakros (the Upper Town)

Where to...
Stay

Prices
Prices are for a double room per night
€ under €70   €€ €70–€150   €€€ over €150

Coral Hotel €€
The Coral, right on the waterfront, is the slightly less expensive sister hotel to the Hermes (see below). Try to get one of the sea-view rooms, although all have bath, fridge, air-conditioning, phone and radio. There is a meeting room. The hotel has its own restaurant, with a sea view, and a rooftop swimming pool. It lays on a substantial breakfast buffet.
🚑 193 E3 ✉ Akti Koundourou, Agios Nikolaos ☎ 28 41 02 83 63; www.coralhotel.gr ⊕ Apr–Oct

Hermes Hotel €€
Along the waterfront from the Coral, this smart hotel has a stylish lobby with a shop, flagstone floors and a wall lined with large copies of frescoes from Knossos. Its 200 spacious rooms and six suites make it one of the most comfortable bases in the centre of town. In addition, the Hermes has a restaurant, a rooftop pool, a fitness centre and easy access to a diving club nearby.
🚑 193 E3 ✉ Akti Koundourou, Agios Nikolaos ☎ 28 41 02 82 53; www.hermeshotels.info ⊕ Apr–Oct

Istron Bay €€€
One of the best hotels on the island the Istron, some 12km (7mi) east of Agios Nikolaos, overlooks its own beach and a beautiful bay. Built into the cliff, all rooms have large balconies with sea views. They are good-sized and decorated in traditional blue and white. The restaurant has won awards for its gourmet cooking, and with its own swimming pool and friendly service the hotel is popular, so book ahead.
🚑 193 E3 ✉ Istro, Agios Nikolaos ☎ 28 41 06 13 03/28 41 06 13 47; www.istronbay.gr ⊕ Apr–Oct

Minos Beach Art Hotel €€€
If your idea of a holiday is lounging on a sun bed within splashing distance of the sea, then the Minos Beach Art Hotel will more than satisfy. Set in shady gardens of olive groves and eucalypts, right on the water's edge, this low-rise resort of stylish white minimalist bungalows is ideal for a barefoot holiday. Opt for a VIP bungalow or executive suite for sea views from your private terrace. The hotel boasts several excellent eateries, spa and fitness facilities.
🚑 193 E3 ✉ Outskirts of Agios Nikolaos, 72100 ☎ 28 41 02 23 45; www.minosbeach.com

Elounda Bay Palace €€€
Overlooking beautiful Mirabello Bay and set in aromatic Mediterranean gardens, this luxurious resort makes for a languorous escape. There's a sandy beach, but the pool is hard to leave. If you are feeling more active, there's a golf course and access to water sports and scuba-diving. Rooms are spacious with DVD players and internet access.
🚑 193 E4 ✉ Elounda Bay ☎ 28 41 06 70 00; www.eloundabay.gr

Eastern Crete

Elounda Beach €€€

This small, luxury resort, with some 260 rooms and suites, can claim to be one of the best hotels on Crete. There are numerous restaurants and bars, every indoor and outdoor facility you could wish for, and a breakfast buffet that could see you through the day.

➕ 193 E4 ✉ Elounda ☎ 08 41 04 14 12; www.eloundabeach.gr ⏰ Apr–Oct

Elounda Mare €€€

One of the best hotels on the island, this deluxe resort overlooks the Mirabello Gulf. In addition to its regular rooms, it has luxury villas, each with its own pool. Rooms are decorated in a style that mixes traditional wooden furniture with lots of marble and all modern amenities. There are three restaurants, golf, tennis and water sports galore.

➕ 193 E4 ✉ Elounda ☎ 28 41 04 11 02; www.eloundamare.com ⏰ Apr–Oct

Bay View Apartments €

Easily spotted by the profusion of plants around, they command stunning views of the surrounding area and the sea. The rooms have bright, white walls and although extremely simple are clean and comfortable with TV, fridge, ensuite facilities and lovely verandas to relax on: a terrific bargain.

➕ 194 C3 ✉ Kato Zakros ☎ 28 43 02 68 87; www.zakros-crete.com

Hotel Mirtos €

Probably the best accommodation in Mirtos, this inexpensive hotel is right in the centre of this little town. The rooms are a decent size with basic facilities, and a small balcony runs around the outside of the building, which all rooms can enjoy. Air conditioning costs extra

➕ 193 D2 ✉ Mirtos ☎ 28 42 05 12 27; www.mirtoshotel.com

Neapolis Hotel €

An eye-catching art deco-style building, the Neapolis has 12 basic rooms fitted out with stripped-pine furniture. All the rooms have small balconies overlooking the street (though noise is not a problem in this charming hill town) and some have air-conditioning. The breakfast is generous, often with fresh fruit added for good measure You may return at night to find old men playing cards in the lobby, or the local priest watching the TV. Charming and well maintained, the hotel offers excellent value.

➕ 193 D4
✉ Evagelistrias Platia, Neapoli
☎ 28 41 03 39 67;
www.neapolis-hotel.gr

Elysée €

Right on the waterfront, the Elysée is a short stroll from the beach and the centre. The rooms are clean and simple; those at the front have balconies with views over the harbour, and all have fridge, TV and phone. There is a breakfast room and a small lounge, plus ample private parking behind the hotel.

➕ 194 B4 ✉ Karamanli 14, Sitia
☎ 28 43 02 23 12; www.elysee-hotel.gr

Itanos Hotel €

This family hotel has 72 rooms in a building by the main square and overlooking the waterfront. The rooms are standard for this price range, and all have phone, satellite TV, radio, bath, air-conditioning, balconies and soundproof doors. Try to get a room at the front for the sea views. There is a large dining room and bar, and a patisserie.

Insider Tip

➕ 194 B4 ✉ Karamanli 4, Sitia
☎ 28 43 02 2901; www.itanoshotel.com

Where to...
Eat and Drink

Prices
Prices are for a main course for one person, excluding drinks
€ under €15   €€ €15–€20   €€€ over €20

Barko €€€
This elegant fine-dining restaurant overlooking lovely Kitroplatia Beach is widely acknowledged as being the best in Agios Nikolaos. The chef serves up refined Cretan dishes with a creative twist. Order Cretan wine from the impressive list and enjoy the warmth of the room and friendly service. If you're here on a weekend, you'll need to reserve a table in advance. Do as the locals do, and dress up for the occasion.
⊞ 193 E3 ⊠ Agios Nikolaos ☎ 28 41 02 46 10 ⊙ Daily, lunch & dinner; weekends only in winter

Meltemi €€€
The Meltemi at the Istron Bay is exceptional. It is one of the best eateries on the island and has won awards for its imaginative cuisine ranging from seafood to hearty but subtle meat dishes. You can also opt for the nightly buffet, which allows you to choose from a good selection of hot and cold Greek dishes. There is an extensive wine list, too. Non-residents are welcome in the stylish dining room that overlooks the sea. Booking is advised.
⊞ 193 E3 ⊠ Istro, Agios Nikolaos ☎ 28 41 06 13 03/28 41 06 13 47 ⊙ Apr–Oct Mon–Wed, Fri–Sat 7pm–10:30pm

La Strada €
One of the town's few good restaurants to stay open all year, La Strada is deservedly popular with the locals. La Strada is serving up hearty home-cooked Greek and Cretan fare alongside tasty Italian pastas and good pizzas. If you're opting for Greek, the mixed *mezedes* plate is wonderful way to begin the meal (it takes a long time for a reason!) and traditional Greek dishes such as *stifado* and *kleftiko* are great choice for mains. The restaurant offers free transport to/from your hotel.
⊞ 193 E3 ⊠ Odos Plastira, Agios Nikolaos ☎ 28 41 02 58 41 ⊙ Daily, all day

Pelagos €€
Insider there are several small, intimate rooms with bright blue and yellow paintwork. Food is served all day although you are welcome to sit just for a drink and a nibble. Seafood is the speciality, including octopus, mussels and of course the catch of the day, but meat-lovers and vegetarians are also well catered for.
⊞ 193 E3 ⊠ Koraka/Katechaki 10, Agios Niklaos ☎ 28 41 02 57 37 ⊙ Apr–Oct daily noon–midnight

Ferryman's Taverna €€
Hearty home-cooked Cretan cuisine distinguishes the Ferryman's, one of several restaurants at the southern end of the Elounda waterfront. In appearance it is much like the others, with outdoor seating overlooking the water and a bar across the street. The cooking here

is of a high standard. Among the most popular dishes are Cretan lamb in red wine and a pork dish cooked with bacon, mushrooms, garlic, white wine and fresh cream. The bar opens for light meals and *mezedes* out of season.

➕ 193 E4 ✉ Elounda ☎ 28 41 04 12 30
🕐 Apr–Oct daily 10am–late

Vritomartes €€

This unmissable seafood restaurant stands out on the breakwater with its name emblazoned on the side in letters feet high. A pleasant seating area overlooks the water, and before you get there you pass the tank containing live fish and lobsters. Make your choice of these if you are going for seafood. However, the menu is not confined to seafood, and it would be a shame not to try the more imaginative dishes, even if they push the price up a little.

➕ 193 E4 ✉ Sfiraki waterfront, Elounda
☎ 08 41 04 13 25
🕐 Apr–Oct daily 10am–11pm

Napoleon €€

Named after Napoleon, who dropped anchor for a night in Ierapetra on his way to Egypt, this fine restaurant serves traditional Cretan food. Situated right on the harbour, between the harbour and the Venetian fort, you can enjoy a tasty meal along with a view of the sea.

➕ 193 E2 ✉ Stratigou Samouil 26
☎ 28 42 02 24 10 🕐 Daily from 10am

Kato Zakros Bay Restaurant €

This family taverna is right by the sea. In addition to the indoor seating there are pleasant tables outside overlooking the beach. The restaurant owners breed rabbit, quail and grouse; the vegetables come from their own garden;

and all meals are cooked in local olive oil…and it shows in the results.

➕ 194 C3 ✉ Kato Zakros ☎ 28 43 02 68 87
🕐 Apr–Oct daily all day

Taverna Akti €€

At the far eastern end of the string of waterfront tavernas, the Akti is one of the oldest and best restaurants in Mirtos. Outdoor tables with blue and white checked tablecloths overlook the beach, and there is plenty of indoor seating. The friendly owner offers various specialities, including charcoal-cooked meats and fresh fish. One special dish is the octopus *stifado*.

➕ 193 D2 ✉ Mirtos ☎ 08 42 05 15 84
🕐 Apr–Nov daily 10am–late

The Cretan House €€

Set along the waterfront near the beach, this large restaurant is a favourite with both locals and visitors alike. The large outdoor terrace is the perfect place for catching the sea breezes, but the inside is equally delightful. Artefacts decorate the walls, while above the bar is a re-creation of a traditional Cretan kitchen. Fresh fish naturally features, but try the range of homemade Cretan specialities too.

➕ 194 B4 ✉ Karamanli 10, Sitia
☎ 28 43 02 51 33 🕐 Daily 10am–late

The Balcony €€

This stylish, small restaurant is on the first floor of a centrally located villa. The menu features creative variations of traditional Cretan dishes as well as some excellent Greek and Cretan wines. The owner, Tonya Krandidou, also welcomes guests who just want to enjoy an aperitif or cocktail.

➕ 194 B4 ✉ Fountalidou 19
☎ 28 43 02 50 84 🕐 Daily from 6:30pm

Where to…
Shop

Agios Nikolaos has the most varied shopping in eastern Crete. Pedestrianised Odos 28 Oktovriou is largely geared for tourists, with restaurants and souvenir shops. There are more shops along Roussou Koundourou and Stakiaraki streets. All round the harbour and lake area numerous jewellery shops sell both modern and antique designs.

Just 10km (6mi) away from Agios Nikolaos, the mountain village of **Kritsa** is famous for its textiles. Here the streets are literally draped with rugs, wall hangings, woven bags, embroidered tablecloths and other traditional handicrafts. Make sure you purchase genuine handmade articles (➤ 103).

On the outskirts of the tranquil mountain village of **Zenia** (➤ 168), on the road down to Neapoli, look out for **Moutsounas**, a very quaint shop and café run by Manolis Farsaris. He sells a selection of wares such as spoons carved out of olive wood, *rakomelo* (Cretan liquor infused with honey) and all kinds of odds and ends.

The villages around the **Dikteon Cave** on the Lasithiou Plateau, particularly **Psichró**, also have a lot of textiles for sale.

Surprisingly for a provincial town, **Neapoli** has several modern gift shops. These are on Odos Ethnikis Antistasis, the main street into town between the Neapolis Hotel and the main square. The shop at No 56 sells traditional Cretan items, such as bells for goats and sheep, baskets, knives, walking sticks, wooden spoons and forks, and traditional high boots.

Eastern Crete is a good area to shop for traditional Greek icons. The gift shop opposite **Panagia Kera**, just outside Kritsa (➤ 116), has some lovely and authentic handpainted icons. They're not inexpensive, but the price reflects the skill and time involved in producing high-quality artwork. Beautifully painted icons, at better prices, can be found at the **Petrakis Icon Workshop** in Elounda (tel: 28410 41669/ 28410 41461). It is open Apr–Oct daily 10am–11pm; phone for hours in winter.

Opposite Petrakis, tucked between the waterfront and the main road in Elounda, is **Eklektos**, a good bookshop which sells not only maps and guides but also fiction, poetry and essays on all things Cretan – and in several languages. There is also a huge second-hand section for paperbacks, plus top-quality gifts such as stationery, crystals and clothing (open Apr–Oct daily 10am–10:30pm; tel: 28410 41641).

Every Wednesday morning an outdoor market next to the main hospital at **Agios Nikolaos** sells food, produce and clothes. **Ierapetra** has a street market on Saturday mornings by the Proto Gymnasio (first high school) and **Sitia** on Tuesdays on Odos Plastira. Markets generally close around 1pm. Cheese from the **Lasithiou** and **Katharo plateaux** is especially good; try the *graviera*. Sitia is a major wine-producing area – the red wines are very popular.

Where to...
Go Out

The north coast resorts are the nightlife capital of the island. In **Malia** and **Limenas Chersonisou**, bars and nightclubs buzz all night long. Among the most popular venues in Limenas Chersonisou are **Aria**, one of the biggest discos on Crete; and **Status**, **New York**, **Mouragio** and **Camelot Club** near the waterfront. On the main road is the **Fame Bar**, with soul, funk and jazz music; **Palace of Dance 99** and **Cheers**. Malia's most popular party is **Zoo**. Other hotspots on the beach road include **Zig Zag's**, **Apollo** and **Babylon**. The **R&B Dance Club** is a fun place to spend a night.

One of the largest dance clubs in **Agios Nikolaos** is **Lipstick**, but there are lively bars in the centre.

Along Sitia's waterfront are music bars such as **Nea Glyfada, Scala, Club Porto** and **Albatros**.

The tavernas around the square in **Malia** old town often stage live Greek music, and in summer frequent performances of Cretan music and dance take place at the **Lychnostatis Open-Air Museum**, on the eastern edge of Limenas Chersonisou.

The main festival in **Sitia**, the **Kornaria** (June or July to mid-August), features folklore dances, popular music, village feasts and exhibitions. Performances take place in the old Venetian fortress, or in the town square.

The **Sultanina** (Wine Festival) follows the Kornaria, a four-day event marking the beginning of the grape harvest in mid-August with traditional

music and dance. In winter, the **Carnival** is held at the fortress on the last Sunday before Lent.

Agios Nikolaos holds a cultural festival, the **Lato** (June to September), with theatre, concerts, dance and festival events. Details from the tourist office (➤ 41).

The north coast beach resorts offer a wide range of **water sports**. **Water City** (tel: 2810781317; www. watercity.gr), Crete's biggest water-park, is just inland from Kokkini Hani. Limenas Chersonisou has two more waterparks: **AcquaPlus** (tel: 2897024950; www.acquaplus.gr) and **Star Beach** (tel: 2897024434; www. starbeach.tv). All are open daily in summer. You can try **go-karting** at **Kartland** (tel: 2897032769), next to Star Beach.

Agios Nikolaos is good for **scuba diving**. Dive centres are strictly controlled and offer lessons and equipment rental. PADI-certified centres include **Creta's Happy Divers** (tel: 2841082546; www.happydivers.gr) opposite the Coral Hotel; **Pelagos Diving Centre** (tel: 2841022345 / 2841024376; www.divecrete.com) at Minos Beach Hotel; and the diving centre at the **Istron Bay** (➤ 127). Diving is also offered at **Vaï Beach** (July–September).

The **Municipal Beach Club** at Agios Nikolaos (daily 9am–late) has mini-golf, billiards, table tennis, life-size chess and a basketball court, as well as water sports. Two riding centres that cater for all ability levels, including beginners, are **Arion Stables** in Limenas Chersonisou (tel: 2897023555, www.arionstables. com) and **Odysseia Stables** in the mountain village of Avdou (tel: 2897051080 www.horseriding.gr). The whole family can enjoy donkey rides at **Kriti Farm** in Potamies (tel: 2897051546, www.rethymnoguide. com/kritikifarma).

Insider Tip

Western Crete

 **Little Treats**

An oasis of calm

On the edge of Chania's (▶ 138) old town are the city's attractive **public gardens** with a smart café, a small zoo and a summer open-air cinema.

Go turtle spotting

Two rivers meet at the village of Georgioupolis (▶ 151) and the estuary is home to **colonies of small turtles**.

Sacred olive oil

The monks at the monastery of Agia Triada produce **export-quality olive oil**; you can buy yours on the premises (▶ 155).

Getting Your Bearings

From the two loveliest cities on the north coast to the biggest gorge
in Europe, which plunges down from the central mountains to
the southern sea, western Crete has some of the island's best features.
These include the two most historically interesting monasteries
on Crete, Arkadiou in the north and Preveli in the south, both of which
played immense roles in the island's battles for independence.

Chania and Rethimnon, Crete's second and third largest
cities respectively, have fine restaurants, museums
and Venetian history. But if your only view of western
Crete is of these busy parts of the north coast,
you'll see just a fraction of what the area
has to offer. The beaches here are
bustling, and some resorts such as
Platanias and Bali are packed
with summer sun-worshippers.
But head south into the
White Mountains (Lefka
Ori), the island's second
highest and most dramatic
range, and that world

Top 10

At Your Leisure

The abandoned monastery of Kato Preveli

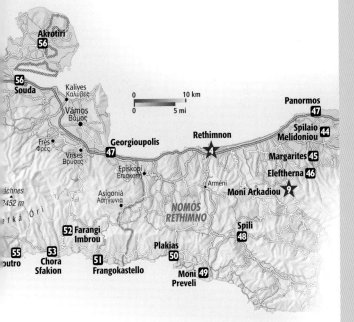

immediately disappears, to be replaced by quiet villages and breathtaking views.

Many people undertake the day-long trek through the Samaria Gorge, one of the most exciting experiences on the island, but other gorges, such as the Imbros Gorge, also make for great walks. These are largely found along the south coast, which is much more rugged than the north. Options here range from hidden backwaters like Sougia to growing resorts such as Paleochora.

To the west are inland hill villages surrounded by orchards, while down by the sea you'll find remote beaches, including the popular but still gorgeous sands of Elafonisi. Spend at least a day driving around this region to take in some of western Crete's spectacular beauty.

Pottery from Margarites

Five Perfect Days

If you're not quite sure where to begin your travels, this itinerary recommends a practical and enjoyable five-day tour of Western Crete, taking in some of the best places to see. For more information see the main entries (➤ 138–156).

Day One

Morning
Explore ⭐ **Moni Arkadiou** (➤ 148) then take the pleasant country road (signposted at the end of the car park) to the ancient site of **46 Eleftherna** (➤ 150). Continue on to the potters' village of **45 Margarites** (➤ 150). Have lunch in Margarites. **Taverna Gianousakis** at the upper end of the village is a pleasant place with good home-cooked food.

Afternoon
Drive northeast to visit the **44 Spilaio Melidoniou** (➤ 150), then continue north to the coast road, perhaps stopping for a swim at one of the north coast beaches on your way west to Rethimnon.

Evening
Spend the night at ⭐ **Rethimnon** (above, ➤ 142). For dinner, sample the food at **Myrogdies** and enjoy the live music, too (➤ 160).

Day Two

Morning
Explore Rethimnon, perhaps spending the morning at the museums and art gallery, or at the Fortezza. Don't miss a meal at the **Avli** (➤ 160).

Afternoon
Explore the narrow streets of the old town, see the loggia, stroll around the Venetian harbour and visit the public gardens.

Evening
Enjoy a relaxing meal by the sea, but instead of choosing one of the touristy restaurants by the inner harbour, go to the **Cavo d'Oro** (➤ 160).

Day Three

Morning
Drive south to **49 Moni Preveli** (➤ 152) and Preveli Beach with its palm-fringed gorge. Head west through **50 Plakias** (➤ 153) and along the narrow, winding coastal road to **51 Frangokastello** (➤ 153). Dine by the lovely little harbour at **53 Chora Sfakion** (➤ 154). The **Livikon Restaurant**, the town's oldest, serves good Cretan specialities.

Afternoon
Drive north past the **52 Faragi Imbrou** (➤ 153). You can occasionally glimpse the chasm from the road, even if you have no time to walk it. Head for Chania, stopping off at the Allied War Cemetery near **56 Souda** (➤ 155) if time permits.

Evening
Spend three nights in ⭐**Chania** (➤ 138). For dinner, good music and a great atmosphere try **Monastiri** (➤ 159).

Day Four

Morning
See Chania's market, **Archaeological Museum** and **Folklore Museum**. Take a break and head to the harbour for lunch.

Afternoon
Allow plenty of time to see the **Byzantine Museum** and the **Maritime Museum** before taking a walk along the sea wall to enjoy the lovely views of the city and the White Mountains.

Evening
Enjoy meal in **Tamam** (➤ 159) located in an old Turkish bathhouse.

Day Five

Morning
Spend the day at the ⭐**Faragi Samarias** (left, ➤ 146). Take lunch and water with you.

Evening
Back in Chania, relax to some live music in one of the restaurants on Odos Kondilaki.

 Chania

The island's second city has been called the Venice of Crete, not because of its canals (there aren't any) but because of its lovely architecture. One of the most beautiful spots on the whole island is Chania's Venetian harbour, especially at night when the lights come on and the crowds are out enjoying the many cafés and restaurants. Behind here the narrow streets of the old town are a delight to wander in, and with its town beach, wealth of museums, shopping and good restaurants, Chania is a joy to visit.

Chania is thought to be one of the oldest continually inhabited cities in the world. There was a Minoan settlement here and modern Chania bears influences of a steady stream of invaders: Roman, Byzantine, Venetian, Genoese, Turkish and, during World War II, German.

A hint of old Venice in Chania's harbour

The Harbour

The greatest legacy is the Venetian harbour, actually two harbours joined together. They meet at Platia Sindrivani, or Harbour Square. Here, the **Mosque of the Janissaries** was built in 1645, the same year that the Turks took Crete from the Venetians, making it the oldest Turkish building on the island. Now renovated, it is sporadically used for staging exhibitions.

Follow Akti Tombazi east past the yachts and fishing boats moored in the inner harbour. On the right you'll pass the remains of the Venetian *arsenali*, or shipyards. You can walk all the way around the inner harbour and along the sea wall to the Venetian **lighthouse**, beautifully restored and a symbol of the city. There are lovely views back over the town and harbour.

Insider Tip

Insider the bastion is the **Maritime Museum of Crete**, which is well worth visiting even if you're not that interested in naval matters. The upper floor has an extensive exhibition on the Battle of Crete (➤ 26). This fascinating display is poorly organised but it shows what life was like on the island at that time, particularly around Chania where much of the initial action took place. Part of the display is harrowing, especially photographs of Cretan villagers being led to their execution.

The rest of the museum includes a beautifully detailed scale model of Venetian Chania, models of ships from ancient triremes (Greek warships powered by oarsmen) to modern battleships, a room full of sea shells ranging from a metre across to the size of a pin-head, and interesting models of famous sea battles.

On the western side of the fortress is the delightful **Byzantine Museum**, whose bright modern displays are housed in a small renovated church. Whereas many Byzantine museums concentrate almost solely on icons, this one covers all aspects of Byzantine culture including sculptures, mosaics, jewellery and frescoes. There are fragments of wonderful 11th-century wall frescoes that have survived marvellously, their colours shiny and bright.

In a side gallery, the **San Salvatore collection** of Byzantine coins includes finds from graves, with lovely necklaces of glass beads, crosses, rings, domestic pottery and a 6th- to 7th-century bronze lamp with a cross in its handle. At the far end, note the icon of St George slaying the dragon. This skilful work was done by Emmanuel Tzanes Bouniales (1610–90), one of the leading lights of the Cretan School (➤ 36).

The Old Town
To reach the town beach continue along the waterfront for about ten minutes, though Chania's better beaches are found west of town. Otherwise, turn left along Odos Theotokopoulou outside the Byzantine Museum to enter the narrow and mostly traffic-free streets of the **old town**, which lies between the harbour and the old city wall. Just wandering around here is a delight. Gift shops alternate with Venetian palaces, many now turned into some of the city's most characterful hotels.

The Venetian lighthouse on the old harbour sea wall

Western Crete

Chania's covered market

Insider Tip Look for ornate doorways, balconies and other remnants of Venetian splendour as you head towards the picturesque Renieri Gate.

Odos Halidon, the major thoroughfare running south from Harbour Square, marks the edge of the old town. Tucked back off a narrow passageway, opposite the Catholic church, is the private **Folklore Museum**, with wax figure tableaux of everyday Cretan life in the early 20th century. Displays include artisan workshops and a bride and groom in front of their bridal bed.

Near by, Chania's splendid **Archaeological Museum** is atmospherically housed in the restored Venetian Church of San Francesco. You'll find plenty of information in both Greek and English as you tour the exhibits in clockwise fashion. Case 10 holds one of the most interesting exhibits: rare seals with Minoan Linear A script, accidentally preserved in a fire, are shown alongside examples of Linear B. Its most important exhibit is an ancient clay seal with a stylized representation of the Minoan town of Chania.

The museum has many other fine objects, including toys belonging to Minoan children, which were used as burial offerings, and magnificent Roman floor mosaics from Chania houses. In a small annexe, the Mitsotakis Collection comprises Minoan and Mycenaean items, vases, pots, figurines, early Iron Age vases and bowls, Minoan metalwork and many other fine items. At the far end of the gallery a central case contains the only known bronze vessel to be embossed with a Linear A inscription, found at the peak sanctuary at Kofinas. It was originally made in Egypt around 1800–1425BC, then brought to Crete and engraved on the island.

Insider Tip Also well worth seeing is the seaworthy **replica of a Minoan ship**, which is on display in a Venetian shipyard at the eastern end of the harbour.

Beyond the Old Town

From the Archaeological Museum, Odos Halidon leads south past the rather nondescript cathedral to modern

Chania. Turn left on Odos Skridlof to reach the bustling **covered market**, with butchers, honey and cheese vendors, fruit and vegetable stalls and tavernas lining the cross-shaped aisles.

Between the market and the inner harbour, the **Spiantza quarter** is one of the most atmospheric places in Chania. As you wander around the residential streets of this former Turkish area, you'll find cobbled streets, charming old houses with wooden balconies and archways, and minarets peeking out above the rooftops.

TAKING A BREAK

Anywhere on the **Venetian harbour** has a great setting and atmosphere, but if you care about your food try the **Amphora** (➤ 159).

Chania
✚ 189 D4

Maritime Museum of Crete
✉ Akti Koundourioti
☎ 28 21 09 18 75; www.mar-mus-crete.gr
🕐 Mon–Fri 9–5, Sat, Sun 10–6; winter daily 9–2
💶 €3

An alley in the old town of Chania

Byzantine Museum
✉ Theotokopoulou 78
🕐 Tue–Sun 8:30–3
💶 €2

Cretan House – Folklore Museum
✉ Odos Halidon 46B
☎ 28 21 05 26 06
🕐 Apr–Oct daily 9–8
💶 €2

Archaeological Museum
✉ Odos Halidon 21
☎ 28 21 09 03 34
🕐 Tue–Sun 8–3
💶 €3

INSIDER INFO

- If driving into Chania, there is **good parking** just to the west of the fortress, allowing easy access to the old town and most of the city's attractions.
- The restored **Etz Hayyim Synagogue**, on Odos Kondylaki in the former Jewish quarter, is now a place of recollection and reconciliation. Originally a Catholic church it was converted into a synagogue in the 16th century (www.etz-hayyim-hania.org, May until mid-Oct Mon–Fri 10–6, €2 entry donation).
- In the Kastelli quarter behind the inner harbour archaeological digs are uncovering the remains of **Minoan Kydonia**. Sites can be seen along or just off Odos Kanevaro.

★ 4 Rethimnon

Venetian and Turkish rule have both left as many of their traces on the old quarter of Rethimnon as they have in larger Chania. Although the harbour is tiny, it is just as romantic, the city's houses are more modest and there are many more minarets. Away from the main streets, many people still live in homes built hundreds of years ago and very few of them have been converted into hotels and guest houses. Another one of Rethimnon's highlights is its 16km (10mi) long sandy beach. It stretches out from the harbour and is lined with several good seaside hotels. There are numerous other hotels along the coast and they are well connected to the centre by the city's regular bus service.

Rethimnon never managed to achieve the historical importance of either Chania or Iraklio. No ruins from Minoan times or antiquity have been unearthed in the city area. The Venetians established the city on a wide peninsula and erected a towering fortress on the promontory. The fortress was also protected against attacks by a ditch on the landside. Today, the spacious inner area is the loveliest park in the city. The city park in the new town is another green oasis that is also used for culinary festivals in summer. Rethimnon is especially proud that it is the site of the Philosophical Faculty of the University of Crete and the city also organises an important annual Renaissance festival. In this way, Rethimnon underlines its claim to being the intellectual and cultural centre of the island.

The Town's Main Sights

All the town's attractions are within the warren of streets that make up the old quarter. You can see all of them in a day, which will leave you plenty of time to shop and to enjoy the atmosphere of a bygone era in the cafés and tavernas.

    The formidable Venetian fortress, or 🏰 **Fortezza**, was built in the 1570s to guard against pirates and the increasingly

Rethimnon's romantic Venetian harbour

powerful Turks. However, it did not hold the latter out for long as they stormed the fortress in 1646 after a 23-day siege. The spacious grounds feel rather like a town park, with the remains of administrative buildings, a church and barracks. The highlight is the **mosque** with its enormous dome and tiled prayer niche. This and other buildings often house art exhibitions. You'll get spectacular views from the ramparts and parapets, but to fully appreciate the Fortezza's size walk around its base beside the rocky shoreline.

Insider Tip

Opposite the entrance to the fortress is Rethimnon's small but engaging **Archaeological Museum**. The museum is housed on a site formerly used as a prison. Among the highlights are neolithic finds, a collection of delicate and detailed bronze vessels from the tomb of an athlete dating from the 1st century BC, bronze figurines recov-

Alley in the old town of Rethimnon

ered from a shipwreck off Agia Galini, and a fine clay model of a small Minoan temple (2100–1600BC). The artwork of bulls and other animals on the Minoan sarcophagi is also marvellous. Among the more unusual objects are a soldier's helmet made from boars' tusks, an ivory-handled bronze mirror of the Post-Palace period (1400–1150BC), and a small collection of red-figure vases dating from the 4th to 1st century BC on which the keen-eyed observer might spot some erotic scenes.

Near by is the **Rethimnon Centre for Contemporary Art**, also known as the Kanakakis Municipal Gallery. This wonderfully restored old building has wooden rafters and white-painted Venetian arches on the ground floor. Although small, the centre has a sense of light and space, and the two floors usually house two or three changing exhibitions featuring Cretan artists. In the streets of the old town a few smaller galleries also display exhibitions.

Rethimnon's other major museum is the **Historical and Folk Art Museum**, housed in an elegant early 17th-century Venetian mansion. The ground floor displays contains documents, letters and photographs on social aspects of

Western Crete

Rethimnon life while the upstairs rooms contain a fascinating collection of folk art, with detailed information panels in both Greek and English. In the large main room there are superb displays of embroidery and weaving, as well as figures wearing traditional costumes.

A smaller room is filled with ceramics and Cretan baskets, together with a potter's wheel and an interesting display on bee-keeping. The next room contains more examples of embroidery, delicate crochet and threadwork. The final room concentrates on agriculture, with scale models of a watermill, an olive press and a fulling mill – a device used for cleaning tough goatskins, traditionally made into cloaks. Picture panels on breadmaking show how the intricate decorated loaves are made for different celebrations.

The old town is full of tavernas

Hidden Charms

Some of Rethimnon's greatest charms are found simply by wandering through the atmospheric streets of the old quarter, where you'll discover hidden fountains, decorative doorways gracing old Venetian mansions, and the over-hanging wooden balconies added by the Turks.

Further along Vernardou Street from the folk museum is the **Nerantzes Mosque**, with its slender minaret soaring over the old town. It is now a music conservatory and concert hall.

Near by, at Platia Petihaki, the delightful **Rimondi Fountain** has waterspouts in the shape of the heads of the lions of St Mark. It dates from around 1626 when, it is claimed, the

The tiny church of Panagia Evangelismos

Venetian governor of Rethimnon was envious of the Morosini Fountain in Iraklio. This small square, packed with bars and cafés, buzzes day and night.

Just back from the inner harbour, the 16th-century **loggia** is one of the finest examples of Renaissance architecture on Crete, once used as a gathering place for the city worthies. Today it houses the **Museum Shop** (➤ 161).

Souliou and Ethnikis Andistasis streets lead up to the **Porta Guora**, the only remnant of the old city walls. Through this archway the busy Platia Martiron, with the large modern **Church of the Four Martyrs** at one end, marks the end of the old town. Opposite are the lush **public gardens**.

TAKING A BREAK

The **street cafés** in the area around the Rimondi Fountain are a great place to relax and take a break from all the hustle and bustle.

Rethimnon
✚ 190 B4

Venetian Fortress (The Fortezza)
☎ 28 31 02 81 01
🅖 Easter until Oct daily 8–8
💷 €3

Archaeological Museum
✉ The Fortezza ☎ 28 31 05 54 68
🅖 Tue–Sun 8–3 💷 €3

Rethimnon Centre for Contemporary Art
✉ Himaras 5 ☎ 28 31 05 55 30; www.rca.gr
🅖 May–Oct Tue–Fri 9–2, 7–9, Sat, Sun 10–3; Nov–Apr Tue–Fri 9–2 Wed, Fri also 6pm–9pm, Sat, Sun 10–3
💷 €3, free on Thu

Historical and Folk Art Museum
✉ M Vernardou 28–30 ☎ 28 31 02 33 98
🅖 Mon–Sat 9:30–2:30, Wed also 4pm–9pm
💷 €4

INSIDER INFO

- **Parking** is a nightmare and the town a warren of narrow one-way streets. On arrival, use one of the large, inexpensive **public car parks** adjacent to the ferry dock or the public gardens (buy parking cards from kiosks), then seek advice from your hotel if you are staying.
- The city's beautiful mosques, both closed, are **Kara Musa Pasa**, at the end of Arkadiou Street near Platia Iroon, and **Veli Pasha**, with a graceful minaret and three domes, set in an overgrown garden south of the town hall at the end of Dimoukratias.
- The **ground floor** of the Historical and Folk Art Museum could be missed. If you're in a hurry head into the garden and up to the first floor.

⭐5 Farangi Samarias

The Samaria Gorge is the longest gorge in Europe, stretching 18km (11mi) from the Omalos Plateau, 1,100m (3,610ft) high in the Lefka Ori (White Mountains), to the Libyan Sea. The trek from top to bottom is long, hot and tiring, rather than difficult, but do it if you're reasonably fit – it's an experience you'll never forget.

The Faragi Samarias became a national park in 1962. It shelters a fascinating array of plants and wildlife, including ancient pine and cypress, wild orchids and dittany, and endangered species such as the golden eagle and the Cretan ibex, or *krí-krí* (▶ 34). This dramatic ravine was formed by a river, which slows to a trickle in summer but becomes a raging torrent after winter snow and rains. Thus the gorge is only open from May to October, weather permitting.

Looking up to Mount Gingilos at the entrance to Samaria

Thousands of people hike the gorge every year, and in high season it can seem an endless procession. Do use common sense before undertaking the trek and make sure you (and your young children) are up to the entire 16km (10mi) walk, which takes 5 to 7 hours – there are no short-cuts out of the gorge once you start. It requires stamina, especially in the heat, and although it is downhill all the way knees and ankles will soon feel the strain.

Take a hat, sunglasses and sun block, as there is no shade for the last few kilometres, and bring at least a litre of water per person – there are places to top up with spring water along the way. Above all, wear appropriate shoes with good support and strong soles to withstand sharp rocks. If you follow those simple guidelines, you'll enjoy the walk and feel a great sense of achievement at the end.

SAMARIA THE LAZY WAY
Tour companies offer an easier option. A ferry takes you from Chora Sfakion to Agia Roumeli, where you can walk up the gorge to the dramatic Sideroportes.

The easiest way to walk the Faragi Samarias is with an organised tour; transport details are sorted out for you, and a guide will accompany your group. But you can also take an early bus from Chania to the top of the gorge. From Agia Roumeli at the lower end you catch a ferry to Chora Sfakion to connect with a return bus. Check all times locally.

Hiking the Gorge

The *xilóskalo* (wooden staircase), cut from the rock, makes a steep, winding descent into the gorge. The mountain views are breathtaking, with the sheer rock face of Mount Gingilos (2,080m/6,825ft) towering magnificently above through the pines. The path becomes flatter after about 4km (2.5mi), at the stone chapel of **Agios Nikolaos**. Baby *kri-kri* sometimes venture down to graze at this shady spot beside the river.

Climb over the dry boulders and continue on to the abandoned village of **Samaria**, whose residents were relocated when the park was formed. The Church of Ossia Maria (Mary's Bones) dates from the early 14th century. This is nearly the halfway point, and a good picnic spot. You will find a warden's station here.

Beyond, the gorge deepens beneath dramatic cliffs and you criss-cross the stream several times on the approach to the **Sideroportes** (Iron Gates). These sheer rock walls rise up over 300m (984ft) high but are only 3.5m (11ft) wide, the narrowest point in the gorge. Beyond, the path abruptly opens out to a flat, shadeless riverbed. At the end of the park it's a further gruelling 2km (1mi) in the hot sun to **Agia Roumeli**, whose tavernas are a welcome sight.

TAKING A BREAK

Bring a **picnic** as there are no refreshments until you reach the end of the gorge.

➕ 189 D3
🚌 Bus from Chania for Omalos/Samaria 🎫 €5

INSIDER INFO

- **Don't be fooled by the kilometre markers**; they only mark distances within the park, not the full length of the walk.   *Insider Tip*
- **Park wardens** patrol the gorge to make sure no one is left overnight, and mules stand by to rescue the injured.
- Get an **early start**. You'll have more time to linger without worrying about missing the boat.
- If your **footwear is inadequate** you may not be allowed to enter the gorge.   *Insider Tip*
- Note that this walk is **not possible in winter**.

⭐ 9 Moni Arkadiou

Standing proudly at the end of a steep, twisting road on the edge of the Psiloritis Mountains, the Arkadi Monastery has one of the finest Venetian churches on Crete. But its striking façade is not the only reason to visit. The tragic events that took place here in 1866 have made it a national symbol of Crete's heroic struggle for independence.

During the 1866 rebellion against the Turks, nearly 300 guerrilla fighters and some 700 women and children took refuge in the monastery. The Turks laid siege to it, and after three days broke through the gates on 9 November. As they rushed in, the abbot ordered the ignition of the gunpowder stores, killing hundreds of Cretans and Turks alike in the massive explosion: it was a seemingly heroic act of sacrifice that galvanised support for Cretan independence both at home and abroad.

The façade of the church at Arkadiou

The interior is richly decorated with wood and gold

Exploring the Monastery

Insider is a beautifully carved altar screen of cypress wood, executed in 1902. On the right-hand side is a large gilt-framed icon of Christ, part of a scene of the Resurrection from the church's original altar screen.

To the left of the church is the **refectory**, where 36 freedom fighters were massacred. You can still see sword marks on the long wooden table and benches. A room above the refectory is hung with portraits of Cretan patriots throughout history. At the far left side of the courtyard you can step down into the roofless **gunpowder magazine** – formerly the monks' wine cellar – where the holocaust took place. A simple shrine commemorates the tragedy.

On the opposite side of the courtyard, the old **cloisters** with their arched stone arcade are very atmospheric. Above, a small **museum** houses historic items from the monastery, including a fragment of the Sacred Banner, so called because after being taken by a Turk during the Turkish onslaught the banner survived and was returned to the monastery in 1870. You can still see the battered old refectory door with bullet holes visible.

The **ossuary**, housed in a former windmill outside the gate near the parking area, contains the skulls and bones of the people who died in the great explosion.

◼ TAKING A BREAK

With nothing else in the area, it's as well that the monastery has its own **café** – simple but fine for a meal or snack.

➕ 190 C3
✉ 25km (16mi) southeast of Rethimnon
☎ 28 31 07 27 31/34; www.arkadimonastery.gr
🕐 Apr–Oct daily 9–8, Nov–Mar until sunset
🍴 Café (€€) 🚌 Direct buses from Rethimnon
🏛 Museum: €2.50

INSIDER INFO

- If driving towards **Eleftherna** (➤ 150) note that the road is the one that appears to go through the monastery grounds. The signpost is at the far end. *Insider Tip*
- Take a close look at the **crucifixes** high on either side of the church's altar screen. Each has a ladder propped up against the cross, and a skull and crossbones at the foot. *Insider Tip*
- In the courtyard outside the refectory you'll find an ancient **cypress tree** with a shell from the Turkish siege still embedded in its trunk. An arrow marks the spot.

At Your Leisure

44 Spilaio Melidoniou

Whereas other caves on Crete are filled with myths and legends, the Melidoniou Cave is filled with the spirits of the people who died there, and it is one of the most chilling memorials on the island. In 1824, while the Cretans were fighting for their independence from the Turks, 300 villagers hid inside the cave from approaching Turkish forces. When asked to surrender the villagers refused, at which point the Turkish commander blocked the cave entrance to stop the air supply. The villagers created new air holes in the network of passages but the Turks were equally quick to seal these. They then opened the cave entrance slightly and lit fires at the mouth so smoked poured in and everyone inside choked to death. A memorial in the centre of the cave marks the spot where the bones of the people were gathered together years later and buried.

Without this background the cave would merely be an interesting natural phenomenon, comprising one large chamber at the foot of a staircase carved out of the rocks. This can be slippery and is also very poorly lit, so take a torch if you can. New areas of the cave are still being explored, and though shown on the map in the official booklet they may not be open.

✚ 191 D4   ✉ Near Melidoni   🕐 Apr–Oct daily 9–6:30/7pm   🚌 Bus from Rethimnon   💶 €3

At work in the potters' village of Margarites

45 Margarites

There can be no better place on the island to buy ceramics than in the hill village of Margarites, where pottery is a tradition and many artisans have their workshops. As the main road winds through the village, bright displays of pottery can be seen on every corner. Several of the craftsmen produce similar goods (bowls, jugs, plates, vases) distinguished only by their patterns and colours, but a few produce works of a very distinctive style and to a very high standard, so take the time to explore the different workshops. Even if you don't plan to buy, the pretty town is a delightful place to wander around.

✚ 190 C4   🚌 Bus from Rethimnon

46 Eleftherna

The site of the city of Archea Eleftherna (Ancient Eleftherna) is one of the most impressive on the island, set in a valley high in the hills between two villages.

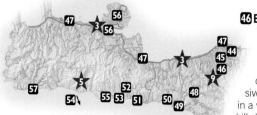

Don't stop in the village of Eleftherna itself (you can reach the site from there but it is a long walk) but go on to Archea Eleftherna from where the remains are more easily reached. Like Lato (► 116), Eleftherna was a major Doric city and later a Roman settlement before falling into ruin. Not too many remains can be seen today, but the setting is superb.

➕ 190 C4 ✉ Archea Eleftherna
🕐 Site under excavation, some sections are open, others are fenced off
🚌 Bus from Rethimnon
🎟 Free

47 Panormo, Georgioupolis & Platanias

The beaches along the north coast in this part of the island include long stretches of golden sand, with several busy holiday spots among them. West of Iraklio the first two main resorts are **Bali** (➕ 191 D4) and **Panormos** (➕ 190 C4), the latter being the smaller but with the better beach. It is only west of here, though, that the beaches come into their own. East of Rethimnon, and in the town itself, are some lovely stretches of sand, with more to be found if you carry on driving west towards Chania. Look for the sign for **Petres Bridge**, where there is access to a beautiful long beach with a few cafés, sunbeds and parasols.

Parking and more facilities can be found opposite the turning for Episkopi, with golden sand running for miles.

One of the most attractive resorts is **Georgioupolis** (➕ 190 A4), with a wide sandy beach backed by dunes. The town itself has not lost its character despite being popular with visitors. **Kalives** (➕ 189 E4), closer to Chania, also has a good sandy beach. **Platanias** (➕ 188 C4) is a large, lively resort west of Chania with a booming nightlife scene in summer.

48 Spili

One of the main towns between Rethimnon and the south coast, Spili is the ideal place to break a journey. Huddled beneath mountain slopes, its back streets are those of a busy hill town, a world away from the holiday resorts on the coast. In the centre of the town on a small square a delightful Venetian fountain comprises a row of 19 lions' heads spouting water into a stone trough. There are a number of atmospheric tavernas that make a wonderful lunch stop.

➕ 190 B3
🚌 Bus from Rethimnon

The north coast entices with its sandy beaches

Western Crete

⓵Moni Preveli

Preveli is not only the name of two monasteries but also of an entire small region where you can spend a very pleasant day. After a long drive through the mountains the road heads down to the **Megalopotamos**, a mountain stream with a beautiful, single-arch Turkish bridge. There is a good taverna here, and this is also where you'll find the start of a hiking path that leads (to the left above the river) to **Preveli Beach.** If you are in a Jeep, you can take the track from here to **Ammoudi Beach** and then the coastal path to Preveli Beach. After the Turkish bridge, the road once again goes up the mountain, passes the deserted **Kato Preveli** monastery and ends at the 17th-century **Piso Preveli** monastery, which is still occupied by monks. Monuments in the monastery courtyard, and along the road between Kato and Piso, commemorate the monks of the monastery who helped British troops to secure their rescue from the island. The soldiers were evacuated from here by submarine to Egypt.

Between Kato and Piso Preveli, the trail

The Piso Preveli monastery

branches downwards to a large parking area, from here it is about a 30-minute walk to Preveli Beach. The Megalopotamos winds its way into the Libyan Sea over this approximately 200m (650ft) beach. Immediately behind the beach is a gorge lined with hundreds of Cretan palms, one of the most important natural attractions on the island. In late summer and autumn, it is possible to follow it – sometimes wading and sometimes swimming – all the way to the Turkish bridge at the Kato Preveli monastery.

🚪 190 B3
☎ 28 32 03 12 46; www.preveli.org Ⓚ Kato Preveli monastery open during the day; Piso Preveli monastery 25 Mar–May daily 9–7; Jun–Oct Mon–Sat 9–1:30, 3:30–7, Sun 9–7
🚌 No buses, boats to Preveli Beach from Plakias
✋ €2.50

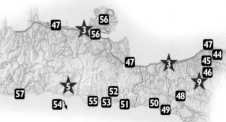

50 Plakias

With its long, wide beach, backed on one end by dunes, Plakias is a terrific south coast retreat for those who want to get away from it all without completely leaving civilisation behind. There are a few hotels, bars and tavernas, and although the resort bears little resemblance to what it was 20 years ago, it's still attractive, with a long promenade, a more remote feel than many other resorts on Crete and plenty to do. A long curve of sand sweeps away at the eastern end of town, and you'll find more good beaches if you continue along the coast to the west.Nestling up in the hills are the picturesque mountain villages of **Sellia** and **Mirthios** – where you can shop for Cretan arts and crafts and enjoy a good meal – as well as the small village and monastery of Asomaton, where there is a folk museum.

➕ 190 A3
🚌 Buses from Rethimnon and Agia Galini

51 Frangokastello

The Venetian fortress at Frangokastello is one of the smallest on the island. Built in this remote setting in 1371 to help protect the south coast from pirates and other raiders, it was also used to keep unruly locals in check. Today the fortress forms a romantic backdrop to the 🏖 sandy beach that slopes gently down to the sea, making it

DEW IN THE MORNING

In May 1828 the Greeks raised their flag at the fortress in defiance of the ruling Turks and in the subsequent battle 385 Cretans were killed. Locals claim that every year, on 28 May, these souls can be seen marching towards Frangokastello. The dead are called *droussoulites*, or dew shades, because they are said to appear with the morning dew.

perfect for small children. The beach is also never crowded. If you want to go swimming there is a second beach (with a steeper slope) 500m (1640ft) east of the sparse settlement around the fortress. This is a lovely spot for a peaceful family holiday. *Insider Tip*

➕ 189 E2 🕐 Mar–Oct daily 9–7 🍴 Several beach tavernas, including Flisbos and Korali (€)
🚌 Plakias–Chora Sfakion buses pass by

52 Faragi Imbrou

Samaria (➤ 146) may be more famous and more dramatic, but the Faragi Imbrou (Imbros Gorge) offers a good half-day's walk through some of southern Crete's most spectacular scenery. It is also more accessible and not as crammed with other walkers. The entrance is just south of the village of Imbros and the gorge runs for

The oasis of palms at Preveli Beach

about 6km (4mi) towards the sea, stopping just short of the coast. It can be tackled easily by anyone who is reasonably fit, and the rock formations, deep sides and abundant wild flowers in spring are superb. Tour companies in nearby towns offer organised trips, which are worth considering, as a one-way walk – even if you have your own car – needs a little organising.

✚ 189 E2 🕓 During the day

🚌 Buses to Imbros village from Chania and Chora Sfakion 💷 €2

53 Chora Sfakion

The main town of southern Crete's Sfakia region has an atmosphere all its own. Its lazy charm and lovely coastal setting, together with the peace that descends when the day's visitors have left, will captivate anyone who spends a few days here. The focus of the town is its small harbour, lined on one side with cafés and restaurants. Beyond here the streets start to rise, some steeply, hemmed in as the town is by the lower slopes of the Levka Ori, or White Mountains. It was through these mountains that Allied troops were evacuated after the Battle of Crete (➤ 26),

Chora Sfakion lies nestled on the lower slopes of the White Mountains

arriving exhausted at Chora Sfakion to await the rescuing ships. Today there is only a small pebble beach, but there are better beaches along the nearby coasts, good walks in the mountains and a get-away-from-it-all feeling.

✚ 189 E2

🍴 Numerous cafés and tavernas line the harbour (€–€€)

🚌 Bus from Chania

54 Gavdos Island

Only around 100 people live permanently of Gavdos, the most southerly point in Europe. It is one of the few islands in the world mentioned in the Bible: Paul the Apostle was shipwrecked here. Facilities are few, there are no attractions, no hotels and the only access is by means of a small ferry that stops running if the sea is too rough.

Many hippies and dropouts spend their – sometimes long – holidays here, camping outdoors or renting one of the rooms in private accommodation. The beaches are good, but completely natural, so take your own supplies. The ancient island bus makes the occasional trip to the harbour, usually when the small ferry arrives, but you can comfortably hike the entire island in a day. If you do walk the island you will get to see the three near-deserted villages in the interior of the island.

🔠 188 A1 (inset)

🍴 Some tavernas (€)

⛴ Summer ferries from Chora Sfakion and Paleochora

55 Loutro

Loutro, with its blue and white buildings set around a cove against a stunning mountain backdrop, is one of the most picturesque villages on the island. There is nothing to do here – the tiny village is little more than a waterfront strip with several tavernas and rooms to rent – but that is where the attraction lies for many visitors. You needn't waste time looking for the road to Loutro, as there isn't one: you either need to walk from the nearest road a few kilometres away, or do what most people do and take the boat in and out. If you tire of the small pebble beach there are good coastal walks in both directions to better beaches, or you can head inland to the mountains. Despite the influx of visitors in summer,

Allied graves at Souda

🧒 FUN FOR KIDS
- The **Fortezza** at Rethimnon (► 142)
- The **Little Trains** in Chania and Rethimnon
- **Horse and buggy ride** in Chania
- The **beach** and **castle** at Frangokastello (► 153)
- **Beaches** everywhere

vastly outnumbering local people, in comparison to most places on Crete Loutro remains an idyllic retreat.

🔠 189 D2

🍴 Several tavernas (€–€€)

⛴ Boats from Chora Sfakion and other south coast villages

56 Souda & Akrotiri

The Akrotiri Peninsula, to the immediate east of Chania, is often neglected by visitors but it offers lovely hill scenery, ancient monasteries and some of the most peaceful spots on the north coast – despite the fact that Chania's airport and ferry port are both located here. The easiest way of getting to the peninsula from Chania is to drive east out of the town centre towards the airport and follow the occasional signs for the Venizélos Graves. These are on a hillside in a small garden, with terrific views over the city. Crete's premier politician and one-time Greek leader, Elefthérios Venizélos, lies buried here, and close by is the grave of his son, Sophocles.

Further out on the peninsula are three monasteries – **Agia Triada, Gouvernetou** and **Korakies**. Agia Triada, with its orange-coloured walls, is particularly beautiful and should not be missed. The others are a few kilometres beyond up a winding road.

Insider Tip

Souda, on the bay of the same name, is on the far side of the peninsula. On the outskirts of the town

Western Crete

is the beautiful and peaceful **Allied War Cemetery**, where lie hundreds of soldiers who died during World War II. The headstones look out over the water, the young men buried in the soil of the island they tried to defend.

✚ 189 D4 Allied War Cemetery
✉ 1km (0.5mi) northwest of Souda ⏲ Open access 🍴 Plenty of cafés and restaurants in Souda (€) 🎟 Free

57 Paleochora

The major resort in southwest Crete is Paleochora, an appealing town with two beaches either side of a headland and a great deal of easy-going charm. Standing on the headland are the ruins of a Venetian fortress dating back to 1279, with a sandy beach to the west and a pebble beach to the east. The south coast can be quite windy, and they do say that if

Paleochora looks out towards Africa

one beach is affected by the wind the other one will be sheltered, but that isn't always the case.

The town has developed rapidly as a tourist resort over the last thirty years or so, and many hotels, rooms to rent, souvenir shops, travel agents and restaurants have sprung up. Despite that, its identity as a town has not been lost, especially on the main street at night when traffic is banned, chairs spill out from cafés and bars, the air is filled with the chatter of conversation and people enjoy wandering round in a very relaxed atmosphere.

✚ 188 B2
🍴 Numerous cafés and restaurants (€–€€€)
🚌 Bus from Chania

Where to...
Stay

Prices
Prices are for a double room per night
€ under €70   €€ €70–€150   €€€ over €150

Casa Delfino €€€
The best place in town is this 17th-century former palace, built around a fabulous Venetian-style courtyard. All the studio rooms, ordinary rooms and suites are bright and cheerful and superbly decorated with old photos on the walls. Air-conditioning (with individual controls), mini-bar, satellite TVs, and marble Jacuzzi baths are standard. There's a large bar, a breakfast room, a roof terrace and a lounge (internet access) – all this right in the middle of the old quarter.
189 D4   Theofanous 9, Chania
28 21 08 74 00/28 21 09 30 98;
www.casadelfino.com

Hotel El Greco €–€€
Perfectly situated on an almost traffic-free street in the old town, just a minute's walk from the harbour, the El Greco is a family-run hotel with only 23 rooms. They are all a good size and well appointed, some being suites with extra living space. They all have air-conditioning, TVs, phones and a fridge. There's a relaxing bar downstairs and a terrific roof garden with wonderful views over the old town to the sea.
189 D4   Theotokopoulos 49, Chania
28 21 09 40 30 / 28 21 09 04 32 /
28 21 09 18 18; www.elgrecotel.eu   Mar–Nov

Ifigenia Rooms and Studios €–€€
Not one hotel but several places close together near the Venetian harbour, all are owned by the same enterprising young man. Some of the rooms are stunningly designed with stone arches, four-poster beds, galleried areas and open-plan baths adding to the striking look. As well as the Ifigenia I, II and III there are the Ifigenia Studios, Pension Orio and Hotel Captain Vassilis.
189 D4   Angelou 18 and others, Chania
28 21 09 91 84 or 09 44 50 13 19; www.ifigeniastudios.gr

Palazzo Hotel €€
You'll find this delightful small hotel on a quiet street in the old town. It was once a mansion and the rooms, named after Greek gods and heroes, are full of wood-panelling and old-fashioned touches, though with modern bathrooms, TVs, fridges and phones. The generous breakfast is one reason to stay here, others being the friendly service and ideal location: use the public car park west of the harbour if you are driving.
189 D4   Theotokopoulou 54, Chania
28 21 09 32 27; www.palazzodipietro.com
Mar–Nov

Vritomartis Hotel & Bungalows €€
Greece's only naturist hotel is located on an unspoilt stretch of coast between Sfakia and Frangokastello. While all the outdoor areas are naturist, the hotel's indoor areas require clothing. A naturist pebble beach, with umbrella rentals and a snack bar, is a short walk (700m/2300ft) away. The hotel also organises nudist boat trips and other

clothing-required activities, such as bus tours and hikes.

✚ 189 E2 ✉ Chora Sfakion ☎ 28 25 09 11 12; www.vritomartis.com 🕐 Apr–Oct

Galaxy Rooms €

Galaxy is one of the most pleasant of the many "rooms to rent" options in Paleochora. The front rooms, above the Galaxy Fish Restaurant, have large balconies overlooking the town's pebble beach and the sea. The ensuite rooms are a good size and surprisingly well equipped with TV, fridge, phone and washing line. They are also clean and well maintained. Though no breakfast is served on site, there are several choices near by. The owner also has more rooms across town near the sandy beach.

✚ 188 B2 ✉ Paleochora ☎ 28 23 04 10 59 / 28 23 04 15 14; 🕐 Apr–Oct

Hotel Fortezza €€

This modern hotel is in one of the quieter areas of Rethimnon, mostly pedestrianised and close to the Venetian fort that gives the hotel its name. It's also not far from the beach. The best rooms have balconies and overlook the small swimming pool. Booking is recommended, even in low season.

✚ 190 B4 ✉ Melisinou 16, Rethimnon ☎ 28 31 02 38 28/28 31 05 55 51; www.fortezza.gr

Grecotel Creta Palace €€€

Although a deluxe hotel, prices are reasonable given its quality and location; it's about 4km (2.5mi) east of Rethimnon centre, beyond the wonderful town beach. The rooms are elegant, bright and clean, and the hotel has all the facilities you might expect including three swimming pools (one indoors), restaurants, bars, gym, tennis courts and water sports.

✚ 190 B4 ✉ Misiria Beach, Rethimnon ☎ 28 31 05 51 81; www.grecotel.gr 🕐 Apr–Oct

Hotel Ideon €–€€

In a wonderful location overlooking the harbour, the Ideon is set back from the main road and has a public car park (vital in Rethimnon) directly opposite. The hotel has 100 rooms, with balconies overlooking either the sea or the private swimming pool. The rooms are modern, with phone, radio, safe, air-conditioning and bath. The slightly pricier suites also have a fridge and TV.

✚ 190 B4 ✉ Platia Plastira 10, Rethimnon ☎ 28 31 02 86 67; www.hotelideon.gr 🕐 Mar–Oct

Palazzo Rimondi €€€

Tucked away in the back streets of the old town, the Rimondi is a small, stylish hotel that spreads over several 15th-century Venetian houses. The conversion has been very tastefully done, retaining such features as the decorated ceilings, while giving the rooms every modern convenience. The 21 rooms are more like mini-suites, with separate living and kitchen areas, and there's a small swimming pool in the inner courtyard.

✚ 190 B4 ✉ Xanthoudidou 21, Rethimnon ☎ 28 31 05 12 89; www.palazzorimondi.com

Veneto €€

Enchantingly set in a historic stone building in the heart of the atmospheric old town, these exclusive suites make for a magical stay. The attention to detail is exquisite, from the pebble floor mosaic in the covered ground floor courtyard to the fountains and water features. The individually decorated rooms are traditionally furnished with lovely touches such as framed pieces of embroidery and handmade lace curtains. The in-house restaurant is excellent.

✚ 190 B4 ✉ Odos Epimenidou 4, Rethimnon ☎ 28 31 05 66 34; www.veneto.gr

Where to...
Eat and Drink

Prices
Prices are for a main course for one person, excluding drinks
€ under €15   €€ €15–€20   €€€ over €20

Amphora €€
The food here is excellent. Fresh fish naturally features but *meze* are a speciality here, and the mixed Greek plate can certainly be recommended. The fact that they use only virgin olive oil to prepare their dishes certainly shows in the results.
➕ 189 D4 ✉ Akti Koundouriotou 49
☎ 28 21 09 32 24 ⏱ Apr–Oct daily 11:30am–midnight

Apostolis €€
This family-owned seafood taverna at the far eastern end of the Old Harbour is one of Chania's best. The attention to detail and generosity impresses, from the half loaf of hot fresh bread and virgin olive oil that arrives after you sit down to the complimentary dessert of tasty preserved fruit, yoghurt, cheese pastries, and ouzo. Seafood-lovers should plan for a long, leisurely lunch and order the enormous, excellent-value seafood platter. If you arrive at noon you'll likely be eating alone; locals fill the place after 2pm.
➕ 189 D4 ✉ Akti Enoseos ☎ 28 21 04 17 67
⏱ Lunch until late

Monastiri €
This outstanding taverna serves tasty home-style Greek food and Cretan specialities with intriguing names like "The Nun's Mistake", a dish of succulent pork chops, and "The Little Devil", a spicy village sausage. Worth trying are the fennel pie (actually flat bread)

and the melt-in-your-mouth lamb in oil and wine. Situated on the Old Harbour east of the mosque, by day you'll get views of the lighthouse but at night there's live music.
➕ 189 D4 ✉ Akti Tompazi 12
☎ 28 21 05 55 27;
www.monastiri-taverna.gr
⏱ Daily, all day

Tamam €€
Some of the best food in town can be sampled at the former Turkish bathhouse, hence the nightly queues for a table by both locals and visitors alike. Most people prefer to sit outside in the narrow street to enjoy the imaginative dishes combining the best of the Mediterranean, from Italian risotto via Greek baked red peppers to Middle Eastern lamb with rice and yoghurt. There's a good range for vegetarians, too. The wine list includes many wines from the mainland as well as from Crete itself.
➕ 189 D4 ✉ Zambeliou 49 ☎ 28 21 09 60 80
⏱ Daily 1pm–12:30am. Closed Dec–Feb

To Stachí €€
The first vegetarian-only restaurant on the north coast of Crete is tucked away in a side street a few hundred feet from the harbour. There are also vegan dishes on offer and even meat eaters will enjoy the delicious meals, as the host is a true master chef. Soups and stews, rarely seen on a summer menu, are also available.
➕ 189 D4 ✉ Dekalónia 5 ☎ 28 21 04 25 89
⏱ Daily from noon

Galaxy Fish Restaurant €€

This excellent fish restaurant has roadside seating opposite the pebble beach, an upper open patio beneath a roof and a further raised indoor seating area. Although there are meat options on the menu, and old Greek favourites, the speciality is quite simple, as the menu states: "fresh fish from Paleochora". Enjoy the wine from the barrel, too.

➕ 188 B2 ☎ 28 23 04 10 59/28 23 04 15 14 ⏰ Apr–Oct daily lunch and dinner

Avli €€€

The best spot to choose here is the lovely open-roofed garden courtyard planted with large palms, though there are also tables on the street outside and in another indoor area. The menu advertises "Gastronomic experiments with Cretan produce and an open mind", and to find out if they succeed try one of the house specialities such as wild kid goat cooked with honey and thyme.

➕ 190 B4 ✉ Xanthoudidou 22/Radamanthyos ☎ 28 31 02 62 13 ⏰ Daily noon–2:30, 6–midnight

Cavo d'Oro €€€

There are numerous fish restaurants cheek-by-jowl around the little Venetian harbour in Rethimnon, and with every waiter trying to persuade you to eat in their establishment it can be very hard to choose between them. It is worth making the effort to find the Cavo d'Oro, which is rated the best by the local people.

➕ 190 B4 ✉ Nearchou 42–43, Rethimnon ☎ 28 31 02 4446 ⏰ Daily 11am–midnight

Makam €

This Old Town taverna is must for music-lovers. Situated in a cavernous stone building with high ceilings and rickety wooden tables and old musical instruments on the walls. There's a nightly performance of some kind, from a traditional Cretan folk trio to a classical four-piece outfit or experimental jazz group. While some come just to listen to the music, most order bottle of local wine, half a dozen dishes of *mezedes* (servings are generous here) and settle in for the night.

➕ 190 B4 ✉ Nik Foka & Odos Vernardou, Rethimnon ☎ 69 38 99 37 79 ⏰ Nightly, from 9pm–late

Myrogdies €

This taverna makes good use of the tangy ingredient on its menu. The red lola salad of lettuce greens, smoked pork, goat's cheese, balsamic vinegar and pomegranate seeds is scrumptious. The young owner-chef Nikos Nektarios is helped out in the kitchen by some authentic Greek grandmothers, which explains how the kitchen manages to produce both hearty traditional dishes (the mother-in-law's sausages are delicious) and lighter Mediterranean cuisine. The live musicians are as enjoyable as the food.

➕ 190 B4 ✉ Odos E. Vernardou 32 ☎ 69 72 69 51 70 ⏰ Nightly

Ousies: Meze & Spirits €

In an old stone building with wooden tables and chairs and a cosy fireplace, this casual local favourite is an atmospheric *ouzerí*. Order three or four *mezedes* per person – you can order more later – and take your time savouring Cretan specialities such as *buyiurdi* – a casserole of layered feta and fresh tomatoes. Try to arrive by 10pm so you get table before the locals start to come in and the place starts buzzing.

Inside Tip

➕ 190 B4 ✉ Odos E. Vernardou 20 ☎ 28 31 05 66 43 ⏰ Nightly

Where to...
Shop

The best shopping in western Crete is in Rethimnon and Chania. For ceramics, visit the pottery village of Margarites (➤ 150). Two potters seeking out for quality wares are Manolis Kallérgis (tel: 2834092262) and Níkos Kavgalákis at the southern end of the village.

Most of the old town south of the fortress is given over to tourist shops. On **Theotokopoulou**, the main street, two gift shops stand out: **Paraoro** (No 16), selling beautiful handmade glass, ceramics and metal sculpture; and **1885** (opposite at No 11), selling handmade silver and clothes.

Roka Carpets, 61 Zambeliou, is stacked with colourful rugs, blankets and wall hangings, all handwoven on a loom here in the shop.

At **Top Hanas**, 3 Angelou, by the Naval Museum, old Cretan blankets and rugs are displayed in an old house.

For beautiful embroidery and tablecloths made on a loom, try **Pili**, 40 Kriari, below the tourist office.

Meli, 45 Odos Kondilaki, is one of the best shops on the island for Cretan natural products. You can buy vinegar, olive oil, *rakí* and wine in beautiful decorative glass bottles, honey and organic olives. At the **covered market** (➤ 141), shop for Cretan cheeses, herbs, spices and other foodie gifts.

Nearby **Odos Skridlof** is the place for leatherware, and though the old workshops are mostly gone you'll find some of the best prices for belts, bags, sandals and other goods. **Odos Sifaka** is the street of the knife-makers.

The village of **Sellia**, in the mountains above Plakias, is good place for handicrafts – there is an art studio, a gold and silversmith and a couple who work with wood, clay and plaster.

In neighbouring **Mirthios** you can find inexpensive, artistic silver jewellery and in **Plakias** itself, you can stock up on natural Cretan cosmetics and local foodstuffs.

You could think of Rethimnon's warren of streets as one giant bazaar. Souvenir shops abound and there is a good selection of clothing since this is the main shopping area for locals too, particularly along Odos Arkadiou.

There are also many jewellery shops around town. The loggia houses the **Museum Shop for the Ministry of Culture** (daily 8–3:30), where you can buy reproductions of ancient art from major museums. For antiques, try **Palaiopoleiou**, Souliou 40. Artistic woodturner **Nikos Siragas**, at Petalioti 2, creates beautiful bowls, vases and sculptures from olive and carob wood. Also try **Olive Tree Wood**, Arambatzoglou 35.

Manolis Stagakis and his son Michalis are two of the last *lyra* makers who carve instruments by hand. Their workshop is at **Dimakopoulou 6** where you can order your own custom-made *lyra*.

Ethnikis Andistasis is the market street near Porta Guora, with delicious foodstuffs. There is also a Thursday **market** on Dhimitrakaki, by the public gardens.

Where to...
Go Out

Most of the big discos can be found east of town among the large hotels. In the centre try the **Opera Club** on Salaminos, **Rock Café Fortezza** by the inner harbour and, around the corner, **NYC-Metropolis**. A number of rock bars are clustered around Platia Petihaki and the streets behind the inner harbour. **Odysseas**, on Venizelou, has nightly live Cretan music and dancing geared for tourists.

Chania's largest discos are out of town, mainly west along the coast at Platanias. **Splendid, Privilege** and **Mylos Club** are always packed. In town, the main clubs are along the inner harbour, behind the mosque. These include **Club Xania** and **Klik Dancing Bar**. For jazz lovers there is the well-known **Fagotto** (Angelou 16), a jazz bar near the Maritime Museum.

A popular meeting place in the summer months is the **open-air cinema** in the public park. If it's Cretan music you're after, there are live music nights at many tavernas, especially on Odos Kondilaki.

For traditional and contemporary Greek music in **Chania**, look for handbills advertising Cretan musicians.

The main cultural event in **Rethimnon** is the **Renaissance Festival**, with international theatre and music performances held in August and September in the Venetian fortress. The programme is announced in mid-July; contact the town hall (tel: 2831053583) for information and tickets.

Dolphin Cruises in Rethimnon (tel: 2831030500) offer a variety of day cruises.

Boat trips are offered all along Chania's old harbour. These include a half-day cruise on **Aphrodite** (tel: 6 9302977292). Alternatively, take a trip on a glass-bottom boat with **Evagelos** (tel: 6945874283) or the **Posidon Sea Discoverer** (tel: 2821055838). Particularly scenic options are the one-hour boat trips that offer lovely views of Chania against a backdrop of the White Mountains.

Limnoupolis Waterpark (tel: 2821033246, May–Oct 10–6:30), is 7km (4mi) from Chania on the Omalos road.

Two dive centres in Rethimnon are **Paradise Dive Centre**, 73 and 75 El Venizelou (tel: 2831026317) and **Dolphin Diving Centre**, Hotel Rethimnon Mare-Scaleta (tel: 2831071703).

In Chania, try **Blue Adventurers Diving**, 69 Daskalogianni Street (tel: 2821040608).

The best mountain bike rental in the Chania region is **Hellas Bike** in Agia Marina, west of Chania (tel: 2821060858, www.hellasbike.net); in Georgioupolis you can opt for **Adventure Bikes** in the town centre (tel: 2825061830, www.adventurebikes.org) and in Rethimnon there is **Olympic Bike Travel** (tel: 2831072383; www.olympicbike.com).

The Happy Walker, 56 Tombazi Street (tel: 2831052920; www.happywalker.nl), organises guided walks in the countryside from one to ten days.

Walks & Tours

Walks & Tours

1 ZAROS & FARAGI ROUVAS
Walk

DISTANCE 8km (5mi). Note that this route is impassable in winter.
TIME 3–4 hours
START/END POINT Zaros ✚ 191 E2

This exhilarating walk takes you to a mountain monastery and up the rocky Rouvas Gorge, rich in flora and fauna, with beautiful views of central Crete's Psiloritis range. Start early to avoid the worst of the midday heat.

1–2
Zaros, nestling at the southern foot of Oros Ida (Psiloritis), is famous throughout Crete for its spring water, bottled on the edge of town. Drive west through town and park on the main road near the post office. (To shorten the walk, drive to the lake.)

2–3
Continue along the main road until you see signs for the Idi Hotel and Lake Votomos just past a modern fountain. Turn right and follow the narrow road up the hill to the **Idi Hotel** (▶ 100), about 1km (0.5mi) from town.

3–4
The road makes a sharp bend to the left. Continue uphill past the trout farm – its fish is a Zaros speciality. After 15 minutes you reach small **Limni Votomos**, formed by the Zaros springs, with a good taverna on the south side.

4–5
Both the right- and left-hand paths lead round the shore of the lake and up stone steps. Go through the gate and proceed along the dirt path that ascends above the olive groves. As you round a bend you will see **Moni Agios Nikolaos** ahead on your

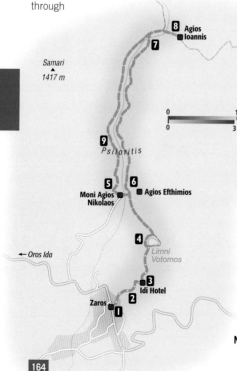

left. Although the complex appears modern, the church has frescoes dating from the 14th century.

5–6

Opposite a little wooden bridge beside the monastery a set of rock steps on your right leads up to the tiny chapel of **Agios Efthimios**, filled with icons. Cross the bridge and follow the path as it turns sharply to the right and zigzags up and away from the monastery. Follow the yellow arrows and markings painted on the rocks to guide you through the boulders. You are now entering the **Faragi Rouvkas (Rouvas Gorge)**, which the locals also call Agios Nikolaos Gorge, after the monastery.

6–7

After a short, steep climb you come to a fence. Go right, following the arrow as the path curves around the next hill. Take the stone steps up and through a gate. The 1.6km (1mi) path through the gorge alternates easy stretches along the herb-covered hillsides with steeper climbs up stone steps. The route is well marked with yellow arrows.

Oros Ida (Psiloritis) seen from Zaros

TAKING A BREAK
Taverna Oasis, opposite the post office in Zaros, is a cheerful spot. The Idi Hotel's pretty courtyard bar, the **Votamos Taverna** (➤ 102), and the **taverna** at Limni Votamos are other options.

7–8

The path follows the steep side of the gorge, then drops down through the ravine and doubles back on the far side. Here it becomes a wide track leading uphill to a signpost. To extend the walk to a full day, follow the trail up through the peaks for 2.7km (1.5mi) to the church of **Agios Ioannis**.

8–9

To return, follow the sign for Votamos and **Agios Nikolaos**. This dirt track is narrow and steep at first, so go slow. There are beautiful views down the gorge to Zaros. After passing some beehives turn left on to a wide dirt road that leads downhill to the monastery. Follow the sign for Votamos round behind it to the wooden bridge, and return to Zaros the way you came.

2 ORCHARDS & OLIVE GROVES
Walk

> **DISTANCE** 5km (3mi)
> **TIME** 2 hours
> **START/END POINT** Limnes ✚ 193 D4

You will often see windmills from a distance while driving through Crete, but this walk enables you to view them up close. Following tracks and quiet roads, it links three of eastern Crete's unspoilt villages while meandering through olive groves and orchards of lemon trees, apple trees and bright red pomegranates.

❶–❷

Driving west to east on the old road between Neapoli and Agios Nikolaos, pass the first few buildings as you arrive in **Limnes** and park just after a bridge on the right of the road at a sharp bend. Cross the bridge and walk along the path between white stone walls, past windmills and vines.

After 50m reach a large taverna, where you turn left and immediately right. Pomegranate trees line one side of the path, olives and figs the other. Further on are patches, lime and lemon trees.

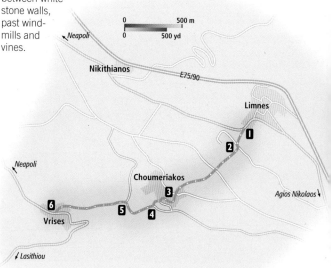

2–3

At the next junction, turn left and immediately right again. The path is flanked with olive groves and passes, on the right, a red-roofed church surrounded by flowers and shrubs. The path goes slightly uphill as it brings you into **Choumeriakos** village, where you turn right, passing a shrine and a memorial on your right. In the village square there are a few cafés and shops. Take the road that goes uphill on the left side of the square, passing the church and an old fountain in a wall on your left.

3–4

Turn right at the first T-junction you reach, then follow the path as it swings left and climbs uphill. Pause on the corner for a view back to Limnes to the right, with the rest of the village of Choumeriakos to the left. From here carry on uphill, ignoring the track to the right. The main track then swings right and carries on uphill, leaving the village behind. On reaching a tarmac road, turn right.

4–5

The road swings right past more olive trees and heads towards a white chapel on a small hill. The

TAKING A BREAK
There are simple tavernas and cafés in **Limnes, Choumeriakos** and **Vrises**.

chapel is locked but climb up to it for lovely views of the land around. Far to the left is Neapoli, to the right in the distance the village of **Nikithianos**, and to the right of that is Limnes, where the walk started. Up the hill to the immediate left is Vrises, your destination.

5–6

Continue on this quiet road until you reach a rough T-junction. The left fork leads up the long way round to the main Lasithiou–Neapoli road, and you can turn right into upper Vrises. If you turn right, however, it is an easy walk into lower **Vrises**, with its narrow streets and whitewashed houses with vine-covered terraces. To find a café or a shop you will need to pick your way up one of the sets of steps that leads up to the main part of the village. Afterwards, simply retrace your steps to Limnes where there are several tavernas.

Insider Tip

A grove of olive trees

Walks & Tours

3 OROPEDIO LASITHIOU
Drive

DISTANCE 80km (50mi) **TIME** 8–12 hours
START POINT Neapoli ✚ 193 D4
END POINT Malia Archaeological Site ✚ 192 C4

The Lasithiou Plateau stands 850m (2,790ft) high in the Dikti Mountains, and is one of the most picturesque areas of the island. The fertile area produces rich crops of fruit and many types of vegetables, including potatoes and cabbage.

🌀–🌀

From the main square in **Neapoli**, follow the signs to the south for the "Plateau of Lasithiou" (sometimes spelt "Lassithi"). The route is well signed almost all the way. The good tarmac road quickly winds up through olive groves and the upper part of the village of Vrises. After turning right,

again signed, you'll see lovely views of the Selena Mountains ahead.

🌀–🌀

The road descends to irrigated olive groves then climbs up the other side of the little valley into a stark and rocky landscape. About 12km (7.5mi) from Neapoli pass through the hamlet of **Kato Amigdali**, and soon afterwards its big brother, **Ano Amigdali**.

🌀–🌀

After Ano Amigdali you reach the delightful village of **Zenia**, a cluster of vine-covered houses. It is well

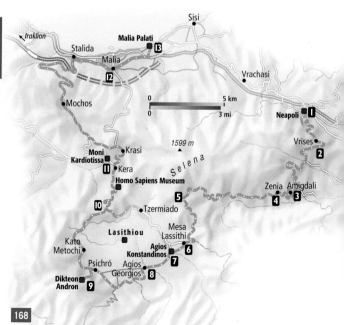

5–6

The road gets increasingly steep as it crosses over the mountains, and in winter when it snows, this stretch may be closed. Beyond is the Lasithiou Plateau itself.

6–7

After passing through Mesa Lasithi you reach a T-junction. Turn left towards Agios Georgios. The first village after the T-junction is **Agios Konstandinos**, where several shops sell weaving and textiles. Here you can enjoy a tasty meal at Taverna Vilaeti. **Insider Tip**

worth stopping off at Moutsounas, a very quaint café and bar that also sells a variety of local produce and crafts.

4–5

The road winds higher now. Soon, on your right as you round a bend, you will see your first stone-based windmill. In the village of **Mesa Potami** a delightful stop is Taverna Marianna, which has one of the prettiest terraces in Crete, festooned in flowers. The vegetables and salad greens served all come from the taverna garden.

7–8

In Agios Georgios, drive up past the church and go to the left following the signs for the **Dikteon Cave** and the Venizélos Museum. Look for a bend to the right where a sign points left to the **Cretan Folklore Museum** and the **Venizélos Museum**. Park on the main road and walk up, as there is not much space to park above. Both little museums are worth seeing. The guidebook for the Folklore Museum has an old photo showing

Windmills on the Lasithiou Plateau

Walks & Tours

hundreds of white-sailed windmills across the plain.

8–9
Drive on out of the village and turn left at the sign for the **Dikteon Andron**. The narrow road passes through more villages. Just beyond the town of Psichró, a sign points left up the hill 2km (1mi) to the Dikteon Cave (▶ 121). There are more good views of the Lasithiou Plateau from the official car park.

9–10
Drive back down to Psichró and turn left, continuing the drive around the plateau. Orchards and farms are still plentiful, with olive groves and cows grazing on the plain. A few kilometres beyond the village of Kato Metohi, the road splits. Ignore the left turn to Iraklio for the moment but carry straight on to **Tzermiado**, the largest town in the region. It's a pleasant old provincial town with handicrafts for sale and several restaurants. After a break you should return the way you came in, this time taking the road towards Iraklio.

10–11
Next follows one of the best parts of the drive, through the Perasma Seli Abelou (pass). Windmills can be seen along the ridge, to which you can walk if you want close-up views. Shortly thereafter, on the mountain slope, is the private **Homo Sapiens Museum**. An open-air museum that is owned by an eccentric Cretan who has some quirky displays that represent the evolution of man from Homo erectus to Homo sapiens and ending with 'Homo astronauticus' (open during the day, entrance: €3).

11–12
The road curves down the mountain – an exhilarating drive, but watch for the sharp right turn to **Krasi**. Look for the enormous gnarled old plane tree in the village, and the nearby spring where locals fill their water bottles. Carry on through the village and rejoin the main road, simply following signs now for Malia. The road curves back up over rocky hills, then switchbacks steeply back down again, a pretty and majestic drive through a dry rocky landscape.

12–13
This road brings you into Malia a back way. Turn right at the stop sign towards Agios Nikolaos to reach the entrance to **Malia Palati** (▶ 114), a lovely place to end an impressive drive.

A shepherd with his flock on the Lasithiou Plateau

4 THE AMARI VALLEY
Drive

DISTANCE 100km (62mi)
TIME 8–12 hours
START/END POINT Agia Galini ✚ 190 C2

The Amari Valley is one of the most beautiful and fertile regions of Crete. Here you will enjoy breathtaking views, orchards, vineyards and olive groves, and experience genuine Cretan hospitality in the lovely villages encountered en route. You can start from Rethimnon and join the route at Agia Foteini (31km/19mi from Rethimnon), thus missing the winding roads with spectacular views out of Agia Galini.

The glorious Amari Valley spreads out below

1–2
Take the main road out of Agia Galini. Ignore the first two roads going off to the left. After 5km (3mi) take the left turn for Amari and Rethimnon. As you now head north you see the southern slopes of the Psiloritis range ahead of you to the right. After 2km (1mi)

a sign in Greek indicates the left turn to **Agia Paraskevi**, which you take. The road is asphalt but watch out for the pot-holes. Olive groves lie on either side, and high in the hills to your left is the mountain village of **Melambes**.

2–3
In **Agia Paraskevi** the Ekklisia tis Panagias has fine 16th-century frescoes. You will have to park and ask for directions as it is hidden away, off the main road. This road winds up through Agia Paraskevi and becomes more gravelly with sharp uphill bends. The high peak on the left on the far side of the valley is **Kedros** (1,776m/5,827ft).

Walks & Tours

🄃–🄄

At the next junction take the left fork towards Rethimnon. This is a wonderful road that snakes down into the valley and up the other side, with many a sharp bend. Look out for eagles and vultures circling overhead. Some 9km (5mi) after the junction you reach an

after the kidnapping of the German General Kreipe during World War II (➤ 28), German troops destroyed them by way of reprisal, slaughtering the men, looting and burning the houses, and dynamiting schools and cemeteries. The villages were rebuilt after the war, although a few old churches survived.

🄅–🄆

About 5km (3mi) after Vrises is **Gerakari**, the centre of the cherry-growing area. Stop at the Taverna Yerakari on the right of the main street to try the

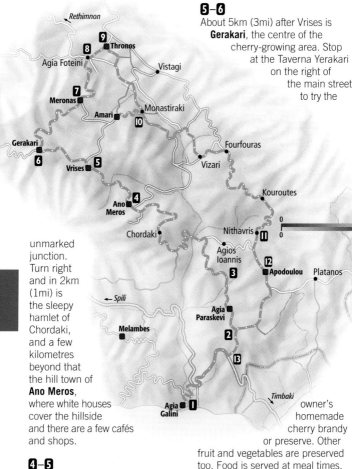

unmarked junction. Turn right and in 2km (1mi) is the sleepy hamlet of Chordaki, and a few kilometres beyond that the hill town of **Ano Meros**, where white houses cover the hillside and there are a few cafés and shops.

owner's homemade cherry brandy or preserve. Other fruit and vegetables are preserved too. Food is served at meal times.

🄄–🄅

About 4km (2.5mi) beyond Ano Meros is **Vrises**, with more shops and cafés and, on the right of the main road, a large white war memorial. These Amari Valley villages may look peaceful now, but

🄆–🄇

Continue through Gerakari, ignoring the left turn to Spili and various minor turns and staying on the main road towards **Meronas**.

In Meronas look for the old church on the right. Park around the next bend where a monument commemorates the villagers who died in various wars from 1717 to 1949.

Walk back to look at the beautiful 14th-century Byzantine Ekklisia tis Panagias with its fresco-covered walls and ceilings.

7–8
A few kilometres beyond Meronas is a picnic stop on the right, with fabulous views of the valley. Soon after this is the village of Agia Fotini, where you meet a main road: turn right, signposted for the Asomati School. After 1km (0.5mi) turn left for **Thronos**.

8–9
In **Thronos** is the wonderful 11th-century Ekklisia tis Panagias, on the right. Though it is usually locked, part of a lovely mosaic can be seen on the floor outside the church, and beyond it good views of the valley.

9–10
Beyond Thronos the road forks. Turn right to loop back down and meet the main road again, where you turn left. When you reach the next few houses take the sharp right turn to the village of **Amari** itself. In Amari, park in the small square outside the taverna and walk up the nearby narrow street that heads up towards the Venetian bell tower. You can climb the tower to enjoy the views but there is no guardrail, so take care. Drive out of the village square the way you came in, keeping straight on past the police station and on through Monastiraki to rejoin the main road.

10–11
At the main road turn right, signposted Vizari. Drive on through Vizari to Fourfouras. Continue through Fourfouras and Kouroutes and, as you leave the next village, **Nithavris**, take the road to Timpaki, ignoring the right turn to Agios Ioannis.

11–12
At **Apodoulou**, if time allows, park in the village and look for the signs to the Minoan site, which is still being excavated, and to the 14th-century Church of Agios Georgios.

12–13
Beyond Apodoulou, ignore the left fork marked Platanos and keep on the main road to the right (not signed). Rejoin the main road and turn left towards Timpaki, then at the next junction turn right back to Agia Galini.

Rural idyll in the village of Amari

5 WEST COAST OF CRETE
Drive

DISTANCE 110km (68mi)
TIME 3 hours driving, 6 hours with stops
START/END POINT Kastelli Kissamos (43km/27mi west of Chania) ✚ 188 B4

Some of Crete's best sandy beaches lie on the island's far western coast, and their remote location has so far brought only minimal development, leaving them largely unspoiled. The dramatic mountain and coastal scenery is well worth the long day's drive. Drive with care on the narrow mountain roads.

1–2

From Kissamos (Kastelli) on the north coast, take the Old Road east towards Chania for about 2km (1.2mi) to Kaloudiana. Turn south to **Topolia**, a pretty whitewashed village clinging to steep slopes. The church of Agia Paraskevi, with its striking Italianate bell tower, has late Byzantine frescoes.

TAKING A BREAK

The **Kastanofolia taverna** in Elos serves good food. There are snack bars with drinks and sandwiches at Elafonisi. On the coast road the larger villages of Kampos and Sfinari have tavernas. The **Sun Set taverna** at Falasarna is a simple but pleasant spot. Most tavernas are closed out of season.

2–3

Just beyond town a single-lane tunnel marks the start of the **Koutsomatados ravine**. Only 1.5km (1mi) long, it is highly dramatic, the narrow road clinging to the western slope with sheer cliffs rising 300m (984ft) above a river bed. Near the end of the gorge, steep steps on the right lead up to **Agia Sofia** cave, one of the biggest on Crete. The huge cavern is filled with stalagmites and stalactites, and there is a small chapel. It was occupied in neolithic times. Just beyond is **Koutsomatados** village with a couple of tavernas.

3–4

Continue straight ahead on the main road through the Tiflos Valley, lush with olive groves and tall plane and chestnut trees.

4–5

At **Elos**, the road winds up the hillside to the centre of this pretty village, the largest of the nine

In the Agia Sofia cave

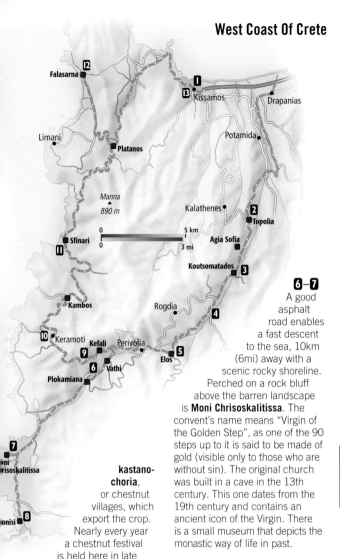

6–7

A good asphalt road enables a fast descent to the sea, 10km (6mi) away with a scenic rocky shoreline. Perched on a rock bluff above the barren landscape is **Moni Chrisoskalitissa**. The convent's name means "Virgin of the Golden Step", as one of the 90 steps up to it is said to be made of gold (visible only to those who are without sin). The original church was built in a cave in the 13th century. This one dates from the 19th century and contains an ancient icon of the Virgin. There is a small museum that depicts the monastic way of life in past.

7–8

It's a further 6km (4mi) to the silver-grey sands of **Elafonisi**, at the southwestern tip of the island. The turquoise waters are warm and shallow, seldom reaching above waist height, and you can wade across the sandbar to **Elafonisi Island**. Despite its remoteness, this idyllic spot is always busy in high season; there are a few snack bars, guest houses and plenty of sun-beds for hire.

kastano-choria,

or chestnut villages, which export the crop. Nearly every year a chestnut festival is held here in late October.

5–6

As you climb higher out of Elos, look back at the spectacular views over the valley and its terraced hillsides. Pass Perivolia, and at the T-junction turn left for Elafonisi. The road curves down a pretty, peaceful valley, passing through **Vathi**, another chestnut village, and **Plokamiana**.

Walks & Tours

8 – 9

Return on the same road, and after Vathi take the left fork through **Kefali**. Its 14th-century church, Metamorphosis tou Sotirou (Transfiguration of the Saviour), contains fine Byzantine frescoes as well as graffiti from early travellers. A path beside the *kafeníon* leads to the church.

9 – 10

Beyond the next village, tiny Papadiana, the road becomes a series of tight, narrow switchbacks climbing up the mountainside. It's very windy here so take care. Look back across the valley for stunning views to the glistening sea. After Amygdalokefali, wide vistas of the western coast open out as the slow descent begins through old mountain villages such as Keramoti. You only realise how high you are when you glimpse the sea far below.

10 – 11

Kambos, 14km (9mi) from Kefali, is a pleasant village with ruined stone houses clinging to the slopes around a ravine. After winding through it you make a magnificent descent into the canyon lined with rock walls of red and gold covered in greenery, and on to **Sfinari**, known for its thyme honey.

Sand and dunes at Falasarna

11 – 12

The road climbs again, affording a stupendous view over the bay and beach below. The big peak of Mount Manna looms ahead. After 9km (6mi) turn left for **Platanos**, a large town of sandstone houses perched on a high plateau. Drive through town. Most signs are in Greek only, making the ill-marked turn for Falasarna more difficult to see (it's better signposted from the other direction). As you leave town look for a blue BANK sign. Turn left on to the small road here. Shortly after the turn follow the brown and yellow sign for Ancient Falasarna. As you descend to the coastal plain, turn right at the signposted junction for Falasarna.

12 – 13

Falasarna has lovely stretches of golden sand set between rocky inlets that are great for beach-combing. Facilities are basic, with a handful of small hotels and tavernas scattered along the road. North of the beach a rough, rocky track leads to the ruins of ancient Falasarna, a port city dating back to the 6th century. Return to Platanos and continue north to Kissamos, 11km (7mi) away.

Practicalities

Practicalities

WHAT YOU NEED

		UK	USA	Canada	Australia	Ireland	Netherlands
● Required ○ Suggested ▲ Not required	Some countries require a passport to remain valid for a minimum period (usually at least six months) beyond the date of entry – check beforehand.						
Passport/National Identity Card		●	●	●	●	●	●
Visa (regulations can change – check before booking)		▲	▲	▲	▲	▲	▲
Onward or Return Ticket		▲	▲	▲	▲	▲	▲
Health Inoculations (tetanus and polio)		▲	▲	▲	▲	▲	▲
Health Documentation (► 182, Health)		▲	▲	▲	▲	▲	▲
Travel Insurance		○	○	○	○	○	○
Driving Licence (national)		●	●	●	●	●	●
Car Insurance Certificate		●	●	●	●	●	●
Car Registration Document		●	●	●	●	●	●

WHEN TO GO

High season   Low season

JAN	FEB	MAR	APRIL	MAY	JUNE	JULY	AUG	SEP	OCT	NOV	DEC
12°C	12°C	14°C	17°C	21°C	23°C	25°C	26°C	25°C	21°C	17°C	14°C
54°F	54°F	57°F	63°F	70°F	73°F	77°F	79°F	77°F	70°F	63°F	57°F

Sun | Sun/Showers | Cloud | Wet | Very wet

April and May are probably the best two months to visit, when temperatures are pleasant without being too hot, there is very little rain, the island is not yet too busy and there is a profusion of wild flowers to see. **September and October** can also be pleasant, but more suited to swimmers than botanists. The landscape will be looking burnt out, but the sea temperatures will still be in the low 20s(°C)/mid-70s(°F). In **July and August** there is no rain at all. Temperatures remain mild all through the year, but in winter it does get wet, it can drop down to freezing in the mountains at night, and it can snow, even by the sea. The holiday season usually runs from **April to October**. Outside this period many hotels and restaurants close. But they remain open in the cities and mountain towns.

GETTING ADVANCE INFORMATION

Websites
- www.explorecrete.com
- www.infocrete.com
- www.interkriti.org
- www.cretetravel.com

In the UK
Greek National Tourism
Organisation (GNTO)
4 Conduit Street
London W1S 2DJ
☎ 020 74 95 93 00

In the USA
Greek National Tourism
Organisation (GNTO)
645 Fifth Avenue
New York, NY 10022
☎ (212) 4 21 57 77

GETTING THERE

By Air Crete has two international airports, at **Iraklio** and **Chania**, although the one at Iraklio is the major airport and much more frequently used. They are about two hours apart by road, with Iraklio best for eastern Crete and Chania for western Crete, There is also an airport at **Sitia** in eastern Crete, which handles domestic flights and a handful of international flights (largely charters).

There are **numerous charter flights** from various European airports from April to October and outside these times there are fights to Larnaca and Rome with Aegean. Most scheduled flights involve flying to Athens and changing there to another flight. There are 20 to 30 flights a day from Athens to Crete in season, with the national carrier Olympic Airways and Aegean Airlines. There are also air links with Rhodes and Thessaloniki. Sky Express, the Cretan regional airline, offers flights to Iraklio from many other Greek cities and islands. It also operates only the flight between Iraklio and Sitia.

By Sea From **Piraeus** in Athens there are daily ferry services in summer to **Iraklio** and **Chania**, and several a week to **Rethimnon**. Journey time is about 9–13 hours. Reservations are only necessary if you have a motor vehicle or if you want a cabin. There is a connection at least once a week from Piraeus to Sitia, on the east coast of Crete, and there are also regular connections to Crete from Rhodes, Santorini, Naxos, Paros and Mykonos.

Bear in mind that ferry schedules can often be affected by **stormy or windy weather**, not only off the coast of Crete itself but throughout the Aegean. This applies as much in high summer, when winds can be strong, as at any other time of year. Always leave at least a day's grace if you need to connect to onward flights or ferries.

TIME

Like the rest of Greece, Crete is two hours ahead of Greenwich Mean Time (GMT+2), and adjusts to summer time at 4am on the last Sunday in March until 4am on the last Sunday in October.

CURRENCY & FOREIGN EXCHANGE

Currency The monetary unit of Crete is the Euro (€). Euro notes are in denominations of €5, €10, €20, €50, €100, €200 and €500, and coins in denominations of €1 and €2, and 1, 2, 5, 10, 20 and 50 cents. Other currencies such as the US dollar and the pound sterling can still be widely exchanged.

ATMs and banks ATMs are common in all the cities, and even in the smaller towns, so you can use your credit or debit card for cash withdrawals. As the local banks charge a transaction fee of 1 per cent or at least €5–€6, it is best to limit the number of your withdrawals. There are banks in all the towns and cities, where you can exchange cash and travellers' cheques.

Credit and debit cards Credit and debit cards are widely accepted in many hotels and car rentals. Restaurants and tavernas usually prefer cash and most shops and petrol stations do not take credit cards.

In Greece
Greek National Tourism
Organisation
(GNTO) Tsoha 7,
Athens 11521
☎ (210) 870 7000

In Canada
Hellenic Tourism,
1500 Don Mills Road,
Suite 102,
Toronto,
ON M3B 3K4
☎ (416) 968-2220

In Australia
GNTO
37–49 Pitt Street, Sydney,
NSW 2000
☎ 02 9241 1663

Practicalities

NATIONAL HOLIDAYS

1 Jan	New Year's Day
6 Jan	Epiphany
Feb/Mar	Shrove Monday
25 Mar	Independence Day
Mar/Apr	Good Friday, Easter Monday
May/Jun	Whit Monday
1 May	Labour Day
15 Aug	Feast of the Assumption
28 Oct	Ochi Day
25/26 Dec	Christmas

In Greece the movable religious holidays follow the Julian calendar and not the Gregorian calendar. In some years the holidays fall on the same date, but they can also be up to five weeks later than our dates.

TIPS/GRATUITIES

Tipping is expected for all services.
As a general guide:
Restaurant waiters (service not included): leave change
Cafés/bars: leave change
Taxis: change from bill
Porters: €1– €3 per bag
Chambermaids: €2 per day (optional)
Hairdressers: change from bill
Tour guides: €3

OPENING HOURS

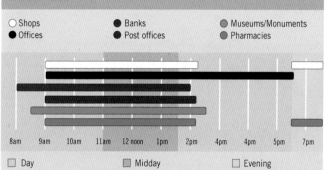

○ Shops   ● Banks   ● Museums/Monuments
● Offices   ● Post offices   ● Pharmacies

8am   9am   10am   11am   12 noon   1pm   2pm   4pm   4pm   5pm   7pm

☐ Day   ☐ Midday   ☐ Evening

Many shops in tourist areas stay open late. In larger towns, some banks and post offices may open on Saturday mornings.

Banks Are open Mon–Thu 8–2, Fri 8–1:30.

Pharmacies Are open Mon–Fri during business hours and on Saturday mornings. Each one displays details of the nearest 24-hour pharmacy.

Churches Churches in the countryside are often kept locked due to increasing icon theft. In the cities, the main churches are usually open all day, though some may open early morning and evenings only.

Museums and archaeological sites Opening hours vary from place to place but the core hours are Tue–Sun 9–2:30.

TIME DIFFERENCES

Crete (EET)
12 noon

←
London (GMT)
10am

←
New York (EST)
5am

←
Los Angeles
2am

→
Sydney (AEST)
7pm

TELEPHONES

The Greek mobile networks have excellent coverage throughout Crete. If you plan on using your mobile a lot, your best option is to buy an inexpensive prepaid SIM card with a Greek phone number. They are available from one of the many telecommunications outlets (COSMOTE,

Vodafone, Wind) and you will need to present your identity card or passport when you make the purchase. There are still public street phones in the towns and villages but, as they are seldom maintained, they are often out of order. To make a call from a street phone you need a phone card, available from kiosks and supermarkets.

International Dialling Codes
Dial 00 followed by
United Kingdom: 44; Republic of Ireland: 353;
USA/Canada: 1; Australia: 61; Greece: 30

POST

Towns and many large villages have a post office, either in a large yellow caravan or a building on the main square or street. Normal hours are Mon–Fri 7–3.

ELECTRICITY

The power supply in Greece is 220. Sockets take two-round-pin plugs. Visitors from continental Europe should bring an adaptor. Visitors from the US will require a voltage transformer. Power cuts happen from time to time.

PERSONAL SAFETY

Crete is one of the safest places in Europe. Crime is rare, although petty theft can occur so don't be too careless with your valuables.
Report any crime to the police immediately.

- Leave valuables in your hotel or apartment safe, never on the beach or visible in a car.
- Women may be pestered by local lotharios, but these are usually a nuisance rather than a serious threat. Persistent refusal usually works.

Police assistance:
☎ **112 from any phone**

WIFI AND INTERNET

Most cafés, restaurants and hotels (except luxury hotels) offer free WiFi access to patrons; there are also several free WiFi hotspots in many public spaces in the cities.

POLICE		100
FIRE		199
AMBULANCE		166
ELPA (Car Breakdown)		104

Practicalities

HEALTH

 Insurance: Citizens of EU countries with relevant documentation (European Health Insurance Card) are entitled to receive free or reduced-cost emergency medical treatment in state hospitals and from doctors who contract to provide services to the Greek statutory health insurer. Private medical insurance is still advised and is essential for all other visitors.

 Dental services: There are many good dentists in Crete, mostly in the major towns of Iraklio, Chania and Rethimnon. Services are much cheaper than elsewhere in Europe.

 Weather: The summer sun can be fierce, and even in spring and autumn you must take precautions against sunburn. Use sun protection even if there is some cloud cover.

Drugs: Prescription and non-prescription drugs are widely available at pharmacies. Look for the Green Cross. Bring sufficient supplies of any medication with you, plus a prescription indicating generic and not brand names in case you need more. Notices on pharmacy doors display details of the nearest 24-hour pharmacy.

 Safe water: Tap water is safe to drink throughout Crete. Bottled water is available everywhere. Drink plenty to avoid dehydration.

CONCESSIONS

Students/Youths Students Holders of an International Student Identity Card (ISIC) are entitled to reduced-price admission at most public museums and monuments. Privately run museums may not give a concession. No travel concessions available.
Senior Citizens Senior citizens receive few if any concessions. Some sites and museums will offer reduced admission if you can prove you are over 60. Sometimes this is limited to EU citizens. No travel concessions are available.

TRAVELLING WITH A DISABILITY

Check first if your accommodation is going to be suitable. Few special facilities exist, and archaeological sites are difficult to get around.

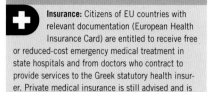 CHILDREN

Cretans love children and they are welcome everywhere. Children under 8 travel free on buses, but over-8s pay full fare. Special attractions for children are indicated by the logo above.

SMOKING

Smoking is prohibited in all public transport, public buildings and restaurants. The ban is often ignored in restaurants, bars and cafés.

RESTROOMS

Remember not to put the paper into the toilet, but into the basket provided.

CUSTOMS

The duty-free allowance for EU citizens includes cigarettes (300), wine (90 l) and spirits (1 l). Non-EU citizens should check their country's custom regulations.

EMBASSIES AND CONSULATES

 UK
☎ 2810-22 40 12
(Iraklio)

 USA
☎ 210-7 21 29 51
(Athens)

 Ireland
☎ 210-7 23 27 71
(Athens)

 Australia
☎ 210-8 70 40 00
(Athens)

Useful Words and Phrases

THE GREEK ALPHABET

Alpha A α
Vita B β
Gamma Γ γ
Delta Δ δ
Epsilon Ε ε
Zita Ζ ζ
Eta Η η
Thita Θ θ
Iota Ι ι
Kappa Κ κ
Lambda Λ λ
Mi Μ μ
Ni Ν ν
Xi Ξ ξ
Omicron Ο ο
Pi Π π
Rho Ρ ρ
Sigma Σ σ
Taf Τ τ
Upsilon Υ υ
Phi Φ φ
Chi Χ χ
Psi Ψ ψ
Omega Ω ω

SURVIVAL PHRASES

Yes (formal) **Ne (málista)**
No **Óchi**
Hello (formal) **Yiásas (hérete)**
Goodbye (formal) **Yiásas (adío)**
How are you?
  Ti kanís (tí káneteh)?
Please **Parakaló**
Thank you (very much)
  Efharistó (párapolí)
Excuse me **Signómi**
I'm sorry **Signómi**
You're welcome **Parakaló**
Do you have…?
  Boríte na moú dósete…?
Good morning **Kaliméra**

Good afternoon/evening
  Kalispéra
Good night **Kaliníkhta**
Okay, all right **Endáksi**
Very well **Polí kalá**
I'm fine **Kalá iméh**
I think so **Nomízo**
I'm not too bad **Étsi kyétsi**
Enjoy your meal **Kalí órexi**
Cheers! **(Stín) yía más**
What can I do for you? **Oríste?**
What's your name?
  Pos sas léne
Be careful **Prosexteh**
Take your time **Sigá sigá**
Who **Pyós**
What **Ti**
When **Póte**
Why **Yiatí**
How **Pos**
How much? **Póses/Pósi/Pósa**
How many? **Póses?**
A little **Lígho**
Open **Aníkhto**
Closed **Klistó**

DRIVING

Petrol **Venzíni**
  unleaded **amólivdhi**
Fill **yemízo**
Petrol station **Venzinádhiko**
Diesel **Dízel**
Oil **Ládhi**
Tyre **Lásticho**
Garage **Garáz**

DIRECTIONS

Where is…? **Poú íne…?**
the beach **i paralía**
the bank **i trápeza**
the bus **stop io stási**
the church **i eklissía**

the post office **to tachidromío**
the hospital **to nosokomío**
the hotel **to xenodohío**
the sea **i thálassa**
the telephone **to tiléfono**
the toilet **i toualéta**
Left **Aristerá**
Right **Deksiá**
Straight on **Ísia**
How far is it?
  Póso makriá íneh?
Near **Kondá**
Far **Makriá**

TIME

What time is it? **Ti óra íne?**
Today **Símera**
Tomorrow **Ávrio**
Yesterday **Kthés**
In the morning **To proí**
In the afternoon **To mesiméri**
In the evening **To vrádhi**
At night **io níchta**

IF YOU NEED HELP

Help! **Voíthya!**
Could you help me, please?
  **Boríte na me voithísete,
  parakaló?**
Do you speak English?
  Miláte angliká?
I don't understand
  Dhen katalavéno
Could you call/fetch a doctor
  quickly, please?
  **Parakaló, kaléste/idhopíste
  ghríghora éna yatró?**
Could I use your telephone?
  **Boró na chrisimopiíso to
  tiléfono sas?**
Police **Astinomía**
Ambulance **Asthenofóro**

NUMBERS

0 midhén	11 éndheka	22 íkosi dhío	110 ekató dhéka
1 éna	12 dhódheka	30 tríanda	120 ekatón íkosi
2 dhío	13 dhekatría	31 tríanda éna	200 dhiakósia
3 tría	14 dhekatéssera	32 tríanda dhío	300 triakósia
4 téssera	15 dhekapénde	40 saránda	400 tetrakósia
5 pénde	16 dhekaéxi	50 penínda	500 pendakósia
6 éxi	17 dhekaeftá	60 exínda	600 exakósia
7 eftá	18 dhekaochtó	70 evdhomínda	700 eftakósia
8 ochtó	19 dhekaenyá	80 oghdhónda	800 ochtakósia
9 enyá	20 íkosi	90 enenínda	900 enyakósia
10 dhéka	21 íkosi éna	100 ekató	1,000 hílya

Useful Words and Phrases

RESTAURANT (ESTIATÓRIO)

Can I book a table **Boró na klíso éna trapézi**
A table for two
Éna trapézi yía dhío átoma
Can we eat outside?
Boróome na fáme kyéxo?

Could we see the menu/wine list?
Boróome na dhóome ton gatálogho/ton gatálogho krasyón?
Could I have the bill please?
To loghariazmó, parakaló?

MENU READER

bíra beer
chortofághos vegetarian
vradhinó dinner
gála milk
hórta wild greens
kafés coffee
  nescafé instant

karáfa carafe
krasí wine
  áspro white
  kókkino red
  kokkinélli rosé
kréas meat
khimós fruit juice
neró water

orektikó hors
  d'oeuvre
proinó breakfast
psitó grilled
tighanitó fried
tsai tea
voútiro butter
vrazméno boiled

MENU A–Z

afélia pork cubes cooked in a
  red wine and coriander
  sauce
aláti salt
anginári artichoke
angoúri cucumber
antsóoya anchovy
avgó egg
avgolémono egg
  and lemon soup

bakláva pastry filled with
  nuts and honey
banána banana
dolmádes minced meat and
  rice wrapped in vine leaves

domátes tomatoes

eliés olives
eleóladho olive oil

fakés lentils
fasólia beans
fétta goat's cheese

glyká fruit in sweet syrup

haloúmi ewe's cheese
hirómeri cured ham
húmmos chickpea dip

kalambhóki sweetcorn

karóto carrot
keftédhes meatballs
kerásya cherries
kétsap tomato sauce
kléftiko oven-baked lamb
kolokitháki courgette
koniák brandy
kounoupídhi cauliflower
kotópoulo chicken
kounélli rabbit
krém karamél crème caramel
kremídhi onion

láchano cabbage
ládhi salad oil
lemóni lemon
loukániko sausage
loúntza smoked pork loin

makarónya spaghetti
mandaríni mandarin
manitária mushrooms
maroúli lettuce
melitzána aubergine
mídhya mussels
milópita apple pie
moussakás minced meat,
  aubergine, potatoes, etc, in
  a bechamel sauce
paidháki lamb chop

pagotó ice-cream
patátes potatoes

pepóni melon
pikándiko spicy
pipéri pepper
piperyá pepper (vegetable)
pítta flat bread
portokáli orange
pourgoúri cracked wheat
psári fish
psomí bread

saláta salad
sáltza sauce
sardhéles sardines
skórdho garlic
soujoúkos almonds in grape
  juice
soúpa soup
souvláki grilled meat on
  skewer
spanáki spinach
stafília grapes
stifádho beef stewed in onion
  and tomato sauce
seftaliá lamb sausage

tahini sesame seed dip
taramosalata fish-roe dip

vodhinó kréas beef

yaoúrti yoghurt

zambón ham

Road Atlas

For chapters: see inside front cover

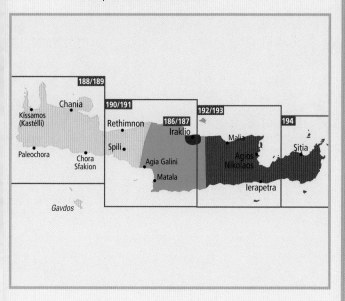

Kissamos (Kastélli)
Chania
188/189
190/191
Rethimnon
186/187
Iraklio
192/193
194
Malia
Sitia
Paleochora
Chora Sfakion
Spili
Agia Galini
Matala
Agios Nikolaos
Ierapetra
Gavdos

Key to Street Atlas

E 75	Motorway	🚩 Ⓜ	Castle, Fortress / Museum
90	Dual carriage way	⛪	Monastery / Church, chapel
	Main Road	★ ⌂	Point of interest / Ruin
	Secondary road	∴ ∩	Archaeological site / Cave
	Road under construction / development	📡 ⌂	Radio or TV tower / Hut
	Dirt road	✗ ⚓	Windmill / Lighthouse
	Lane	Ⓒ ⚓	Campground / (Swimming) beach
	Path	⚑ ⚓	Windsurfing / Waterskiing
	Ferry	⚓ ⚓	Wreck / Lookout point
	Province boundary	▲ ·	Mountain peak / Geodetic point
	National park, Nature Reserve	★	TOP 10
	Restricted area	33	Don't Miss
✈ ⚓	Airport / Harbour; Marina	22	At Your Leisure

1 : 420.000

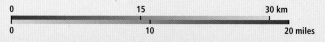

0	15	30 km
0	10	20 miles

Iraklio/Heraklion

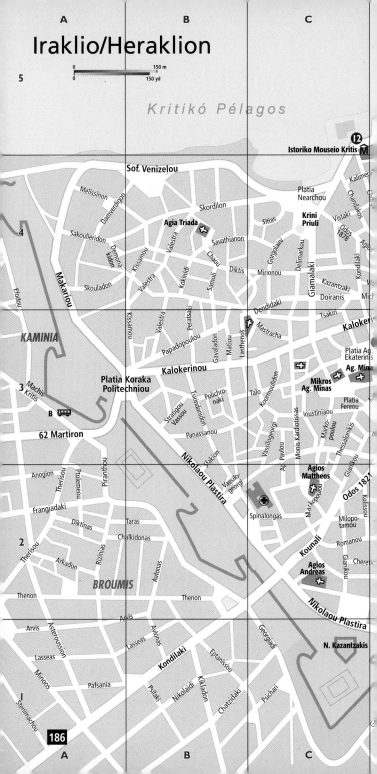

Kritikó Pélagos

Istoriko Mouseio Kritis ⑫ Ⓜ

Sof. Venizelou

Melissinon
Damverdigon
Skordilon
Platia
Nearchou
Kalimera

Sakoulieridon
Agia Triada ✞
Savathianon
Sitias
Krini
Priuli
Vistaki
Chandakos
Chou

Skouladon
Demonakidon
Valestra
Kokkinidi
Chaou
Diktis
Gorgolaini
Delimarkou
Giamalaki
Odos 1878
Agios
Kondilaki

Makariou
Kissamou
Valestra
Samoli
Mirionou
Kazantzaki
Doiranis
Via
Mich

Efodou
Dendidaki
Tsakiri

KAMINIA
Kissamou
Valestra
Peratsaki
Mathou
Lasthenos
Mastracha
Kalokeri

Papadopoulou
Gavaladon
✚
Platia Ag.
Ekaterinis

Machis
Kritis
Platia Koraka
Politechniou
Kalokerinou
Polichronaki
Talo
✚
Mikros
Ag. Minas
Ag. Mina ✞

Ⓑ 🚋
Tsindaridon
Stratigou
Vassou
Kourmoulidon
Ioustiniou
Platia
Fereou

62 Martiron
Panassanou
Sfakion
Vassilogeorgi
Ag. Pavlou
Monis Kardiotissas
Markopoulou
Thessalonikis

Anogion
Therisou
Polemou
Pianthou
Nikolaou Plastira
Agios
Mattheos ✞
Odos 1821
Giamou
Kolissou

Frangiadaki
Diktinas
Taras
Chalkidonas
Vassilogeorgi
Markopoulou
Milopotamou

Therisou
Riziniou
Spinalongas ✚
Romanou
Giamkou
Chereticc

Arkadon
Avlonas
Kounali
Agios
Andreas ✞

BROUMIS
Thenon
Thenon
Nikolaou Plastira

Arvis
Arvis
Avlonas
Georgiadi
N. Kazantzakis

Asterousson
Lasseas
Kondilaki
Epanissou

Lasseas
Psilaki
Nikolaidi
Kikladon
Chatzidaki
Psichari

Minoos
Pafsania

Stenimachou

186

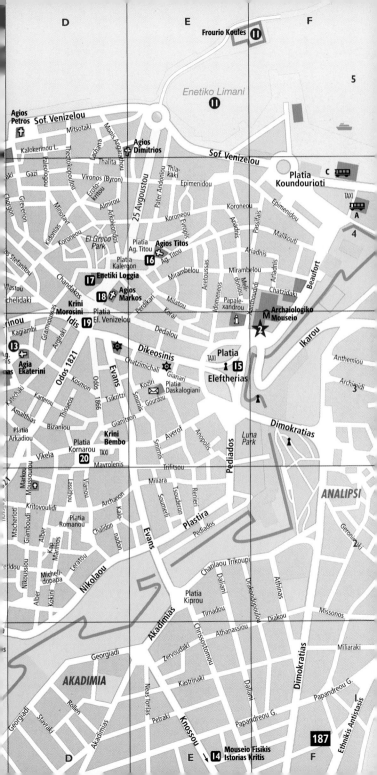

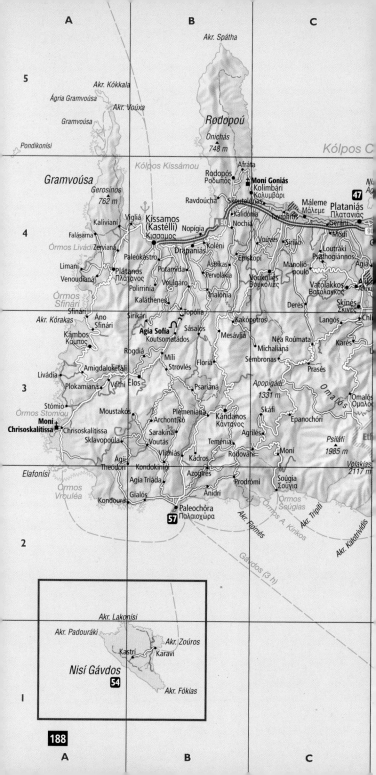

A

5
Akr. Kókkala
Ágria Gramvoúsa
Akr. Voúxa
Gramvoúsa
Pondikonísi

Gramvoúsa
Gerosínos
762 m

4
Kaliviáni
Vigliá
Kíssamos (Kastélli)
Κίσσαμος
Nopigía
Falásarna
Zervianá
Órmos Livádi
Paleókastro
Koléni
Limáni
Plátanos
Πλάτανος
Potamída
Astrikás
Venoudianá
Vóulgáro
Pervolákia
Órmos Sfinári
Polirrínia
Thalónia
Kaláthenes

3
Akr. Kórakas
Áno Sfinári
Sfinári
Sirikári
Topólia
Kakópetros
Kámbos
Κάμπος
Agía Sofía
Koutsomatádos
Sásalos
Mesávliá
Néa Roúmata
Livádia
Rogdiá
Mili
Floriá
Sémbronas
Amigdalokefáli
Véthi
Élos
Strovlés
Prasés
Plokamianá
Psariana
Apopigádi
1331 m
Skáfi
Epanochóri
Órmos Stomíou
Moustakós
Archontikó
Plemeniana
Kándanos
Κάντανος
Moní Chrisoskalítissa
Chrisoskalítissa
Sarakína
Voutás
Agilés
Psiláfi
1985 m
Sklavopoúla
Vlithiás
Teménia
Moní
Agii Theódori
Kádros
Rodováni
Volakiás
2117 m
Elafonísi
Kondokinígi
Azogirés
Órmos Vrouléa
Agía Triáda
Anidri
Prodrómi
Soúgia
Σούγια
Kondoúra
Gialós
57
Paleochóra
Παλαιοχώρα
Órmos Soúgias
Akr. Flomés
Órmos A. Kírikos
Akr. Tripití
Akr. Kalothivídis

2
Gávdos (3 h)

Akr. Lakonísi
Akr. Padouráki
Akr. Zoúros
Kastrí
Karaví
Nisí Gávdos
54
Akr. Fókias

1

Rodopoú
Akr. Spátha
Onichás
748 m
Kólpos Kíssamou
Rodopós
Ραδωπός
Afráta
Moní Goniás
Kolimbári
Κολυμβάρι
Ravdoúchá
Skouteláras
Kalidónia
Nochia
Máleme
Μάλεμε
47
Plataniás
Πλατανιάς
Geráni
Módi
Voúnes
Sirilió
Loutráki
Psathogiánnos
Dragianiás
Episkopí
Manolió-poulo
Voukoliés
Βουκολιές
Vatólakkos
Βατόλακκος
Skinés
Σκινές
Derés
Langós
Karés
Michalianá
Oma los
Omalós
Ωμαλός

Kólpos C
Máleme
Ág
A 90

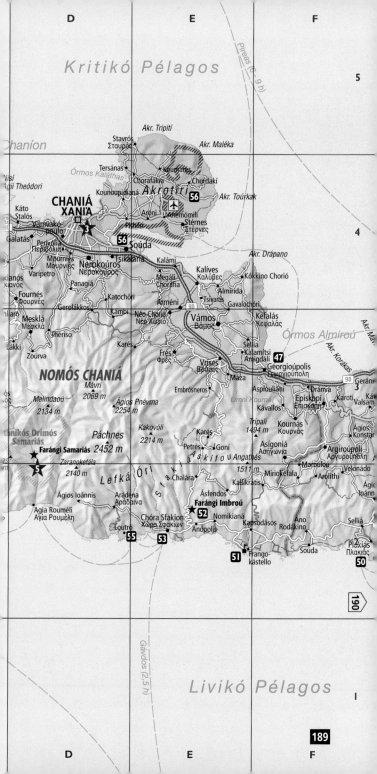

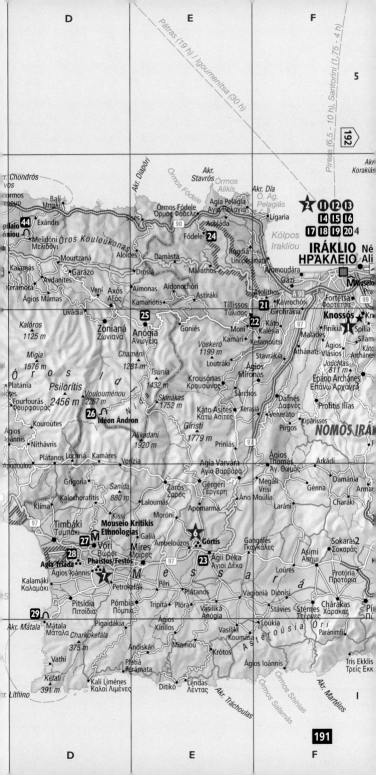

5

192

Pátras (19 h) / Igoumenítsa (30 h)

Píreas (6.5 – 10 h), Santoríni (1.75 – 4 h)

r. Chondrós
vos
rmos
nou

Bali
Μπαλί

Exándis

Ákr. Dianóri

Órmos Fódele

Ákr. Stavrós

Órmos Alikís

Ormos Fódele

Ákr. Día
Ó. Ag. Pelagiás

Ákr. Korakiás

2 **11** **12** **13**
14 **15** **16**
17 **18** **19** **20** **4**

pláio
níou

44

Melidóni
Μελιδόνι

Óros Kouloúkonas

Aloídes

Órmos Fódele
Όρμος Φόδελε

Achláda

Agía Pelagía
Αγία Πελαγία

Lígaria

Kólpos Iraklíou

IRÁKLIO
ΗΡΑΚΛΕΙΟ

Né Ali

Kalamás

Mourtzaná

Fódele **24**

Damásta

Rogdiá
Linopéramata

Aromoudára

Gázi

A 90

Mouseío
Pra

Avdanítes

Garázo

Drosiá

Maráthos

Keramotá

Ágios Mámas

Livádia

Veni
Axós
Αξός

Aïmonas

Aïdonochóri

Astiráki

Afolíthos

Kavrochóri

Girofirákia

Forteťsa
Φορτέτσα

99

Kamariótis

Tíllissos
Τύλισσος

21

Káto
Kalésia

Knossós

Finikiá

Museío

Spília
Sillam

Kalóros
1125 m

Zonianá
Ζωνιανά

25

Anógia
Ανώγεια

Goniés

Moni **22**

Kamári

Keramoútsi

Maládes

Athánat

Ágios
Archánes

Káto
Archáne

Migía
1576 m

Chaméni
1281 m

Voskeró
1199 m

Stavrákia

Ágios
Mironas

Dafnés
Δαφνές

Jouchtas
811 m

Épano Archánes
Επάνω Αρχάνες

Óros Ída

Platánia
ates

Psilorítis

Fourfourás
Φουρφουράς

2456 m

Voulouménou
2267 m

Tsunia
1432 m

Loutráki

Krousónas
Κρουσώνας

Sárchos

Kerasiá

Venerato

Pírgos

Profítis Ilías

Kiparíssos

NOMÓS IRÁ

Kouroútes

Ágios
Ioánnis

Nithávris

26

Idéon Ándron

Skinákas
1752 m

Káto Asítes
Κάτω Ασίτες

Girísti
1779 m

Priniás

97

Plátanos Lochriá

Kamáres

Alikadani
1920 m

Vonizia

Agía Varvára
Αγία Βαρβάρα

Ágios
Thomás
Αγ. Θωμάς

Arkádi

Damánia

Armat

Charáki

Grigoriá

Sanida
880 m

Zarós
Ζαρός

Gérgeri
Γέργερη

Megáli
Vrísi

Génna

Kalochorafítis

Laloumás

Moróni

Áno Moúlia

Laráni

Klíma

Kíssi

Mouseío Kritikís
Ethnologias

Galiá

Apomarmá

Timbáki
Τυμπάκι

27

M

Vori
Βώρι

Mires
Μοίρες

Ambeloúzos

6

Górtis

Gangáles
Γκαγκάλες

Asími
Ασήμι

Sokarás2
Σοκαράς

Agía Triáda

28

Phaistós/Festós

23

Ágii Déka
Άγιοι Δέκα

Vagioniá

Dionísi

Loúres

Protória
Προτόρια

Ágios Ioánnis

Kalamáki
Καλαμάκι

Petrokefáli

Péri

Plátanos

Pitsídia
Πιτσίδια

Pómbia
Πόμπια

Tripíta

Plóra

Vasiliki
Anógia

Stávies

Stérnes
Στέρνες

Charákas
Χάρακας

Pí
Π!

29

Ákr. Mátala

Mátala
Μάταλα

Charkokefála
375 m

Pigaidákia

Ágios
Kírillos

Vasiliki
Koumása

Loúkia

Asteroúsia Óri

Paránimfi

Vathí

Kéfali
391 m

Andiskári

Platiá
Pérama

Miamoú

Krótos

Ágios Ioánnis

r. Líthino

Kalí Liménes
Καλοί Λιμένες

Ditikó

Léndas
Λέντας

Ákr. Tráchoulas

Órmos Shínias

Órmos Salamás

Ákr. Martélos

Tris Ekklis
Τρεις Εκκ

I

191

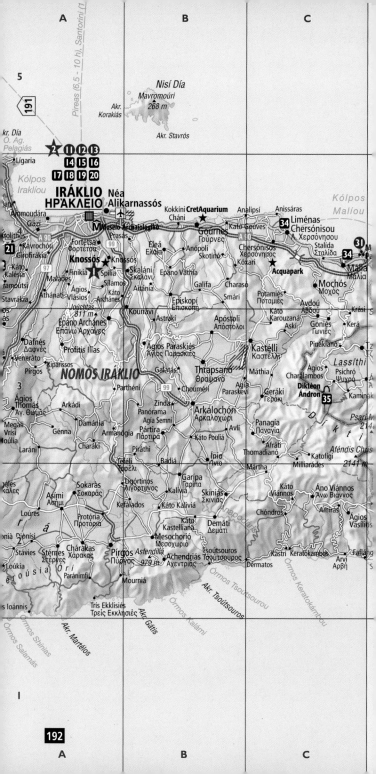

Pireas (6.5 – 10 h), Santoríni (1

Nisí Día
Mavromoúri
268 m
Akr.
Korakiás

Akr. Stavrós

191

kr. Día
O. Ag.
Pelagiás

Ligaría

Kólpos
Iraklíou

Kólpos
Malíou

2 11 12 13
14 15 16
17 18 19 20

IRÁKLIO Néa
ΗΡΆΚΛΕΙΟ Alikarnassós

Kokkíni CretAquarium
Cháni

Analipsí
Anissáras

Amoudára
Gázi

Museo Archaiologikó
Prasás

Eleá
Ελαία

Anópoli
Skotinó

Gournes
Γούρνες
Káto Gouves

34 Liménas
Chersónisou
Χερσονήσου
Stalída
Σταλίδα

rolithos

A 90

Fortetsa
Φορτέτσα

21 Kávrochóri
Girofrákia

99

Chersónisos
Χερσόνησος
Kóxari

Acquapark

31 M

Knossós Knossós

Skaláni
Σκαλάνι

34 Mália
Μάλια

Káto
Kalésia
ramoútsi

Finikía

Maládes

Spiliá

Epáno Váthia

Mochós
Μοχός

Stavrákia
ás

Athánati

Agios
Vlásios

Silamos

Káto
Archánes
Aïtánia

Galifa

Charasó

Smári

Potamiés
Ποταμιές

Avdoú
Αβδού

Krási

Jouchtas
811 m

Kounávi

Episkopí
Επισκοπή

Apóstoli
Απόστολοι

Káto
Karouzaná
Aski

Goniés
Γωνιές

Kerá

Dafnés
Δαφνές

Epáno Archanes
Επάνω Αρχάνες

Astráki

Pináklano

Tz

Venerátο

Profítis Ilías

Agios Paraskiés
Άγιος Παρασκιές

Lassíthi
Psichró
Ψυχρό

Kiparíssos

Galatás

Thrapsanó
Θραψανό

Mathia

Agios
Charálambos

Pírgos

NOMOS IRÁKLIO

Parthéni

99

Chouméri

Agia
Paraskeví

Geráki
Γεράκι

Diktéon
Ándron

35

Kamináki

Agios
Thomás
Αγ. Θωμάς

Arkádi

Zínda
Panórama
Agia Semni

Arkalochóri
Αρκαλοχώρι

Panagia
Παναγία

Afráti

D
i
k
t
i

Psarí

Af*

214

Megáli
Vrísi
 loúlia

Damánia

Pártira
Πάρτιρα

Avlí

Káto Pouliá

Afendis Chris
2141 m

Génna

Armanógia

Piráthi

Thomadianó

Katofígi
Milliarádes

Laráni

Charáki

Tefeli
Τεφέλι

Badiá

Ínio
Ίνιο

Mártha

jáles
kales

Asími
Ασήμι

Sokarás
Σοκαράς

Ligórtinos
Λιγόρτινος

Garípa
Γαρίπα

Kaliviá

Skiniás
Σκινιάς

Káto
Viánnos

Áno Viánnos
Άνω Βιάννος

Loúres

Protória
Προτόρια

Kefalados

Káto Kaliviá

Chóndros

Amiras

Agios
Vasílios

nià Dionísi

r   á

Stávies

Stérnes
Στέρνες

Charákas
Χαράκας

Pírgos
Πύργος

Astendilá
979 m

Mesochorió
Μεσοχωριό

Kastellianá
Κάτο

Demáti
Δεμάτι

Tsoútsouros
Τσούτσουρος

Kástri

Keratókambos

Arví
Αρβή

Loúkia

Óri

Achendriás
Αχεντριάς

Dérmatos

ούσία

Paránimfi

Mourniá

Akr. Tsoútsourou

Ormos Keratokámbou

Ioánnis

Tris Ekklisiés
Τρείς Εκκλησιές

Akr. Gáïtis

Ormos Kalámi

Ormos Tsoútsourou

Akr. Martélos

Ormos Salamás

I

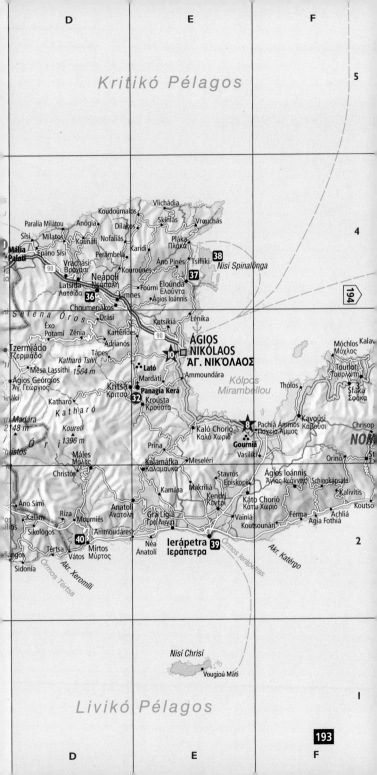

Kritikó Pélagos

- Koudoúmalos
- Vlichádia
- Paralía Milátou
- Anógia
- Dilakos
- Skiniás
- Vrouchás
- Sísi
- Mílatos
- Kounáli
- Nofaliás
- Peri
- Epáno Sísi
- **Mália Paláti**
- Vrachási
  Βραχάσι
- Karidi
- Áno Pinés
- Tsiflíki
- *Nisí Spinalónga*
- Neápoli
  Νεάπολη
- Kouroúnes
- Eloúnda
  Ελούντα
- Latsída
  Λατσίδα
- Foúrni
- Ágios Ioánnis
- Limnes
- Choumeriákos
- Drási
- Lénika
- *Seléna Óros*
- Éxo Potamí
- Zénia
- Kartéfides
- Katsikiá
- Adrianós
- **ÁGIOS NIKÓLAOS**
  ΑΓ. ΝΙΚΟΛΑΟΣ
- **Tzermiádo**
  Τζερμιάδο
- *Katharó Tsivi*
- Tápes
- Ammoundára
- Mésa Lassíthi *1564 m*
- Ágios Geórgios
  Αγ. Γεώργιος
- **Lató**
- Mardáti
- *Kólpos Mirambéllou*
- Móchlos
  Μόχλος
- Kalav
- Tourloti
  Τουρλωτή
- **Kritsá**
  Κριτσά
- **Panagía Kerá**
- Thólos
- Sfáka
  Σφάκα
- Katharó
- Kroústa
  Κρούστα
- *Katharó*
- Kavoúsi
  Καβούσι
- Chrisop
- **Madára**
  2148 m
- *Kourell*
  i 1396 m
- **8**
- Kaló Chorió
  Καλό Χωριό
- Pachiá Ámmos
  Παχειά Άμμος
- ristos
- **Óri**
- **Gourniá**
- **NO**
- Máles
  Μάλες
- Prína
- Vasilikí
- Orinó
- S1
- Christós
- Kalamáfka
  Καλαμαύκα
- Meseléri
- Stavrós
  Episkopí
- Ágios Ioánnis
  Άγιος Ιωάννης
- Schinokápsala
- Áno Símí
- Makrilia
- Kalívitis
- Kaláma
- Kamára
- Kendrí
  Κεντρί
- Koutso
- Ríza
- Mourniés
- Kato Choriό
  Κάτω Χωριό
- Férma
- Achliá
- Sikológos
- Anatoli
  Ανατολή
- Gra Ligiá
  Γρα Λυγιά
- Vainiá
- Agia Fothiá
- **40**
- Ammoúdares
- Koutsounári
- Tértsa
- Mírtos
  Μύρτος
- Néa
  Anatolí
- **Ierápetra**
  Ιεράπετρα
- **39**
- *Ormos Ierápetras*
- Vátos
- *Akr. Katérgo*
- Sidonía
- *Ormos Tértsa*
- *Akr. Xeromili*

Nisí Chrisí

- Vougioú Máti

Livikó Pélagos

193

Index

Index

Index

Picture Credits

Credits

1st Edition 2016

Worldwide Distribution: Marco Polo Travel Publishing Ltd
Pinewood, Chineham Business Park
Crockford Lane, Chineham
Basingstoke, Hampshire RG24 8AL, United Kingdom.
© MAIRDUMONT GmbH & Co. KG, Ostfildern

Authors: Donna Dailey, Mike Gerrard, Laura Dunston, Klaus Bötig
Editor: Bintang Buchservice GmbH (Jessika Zollickhofer),
www.bintang-berlin.de
Revised editing and translation: Margaret Howie, www.fullproof.co.za
Program supervisor: Birgit Borowski
Chief editor: Rainer Eisenschmid

Cartography: © MAIRDUMONT GmbH & Co. KG, Ostfildern
3D-illustrations: jangled nerves, Stuttgart

Printed in China

Despite all of our authors' thorough research, errors can creep in.
The publishers do not accept any liability for this. Whether you
want to praise us, alert us to errors or give us a personal tip –
please don't hesitate to email or post to:

MARCO POLO Travel Publishing Ltd
Pinewood, Chineham Business Park
Crockford Lane, Chineham
Basingstoke, Hampshire RG24 8AL
United Kingdom
Email: sales@marcopolouk.com

FSC
www.fsc.org
MIX
Paper from
responsible sources
FSC® C020056

10 REASONS
TO COME BACK AGAIN

1. Crete has managed to remain **authentic**, despite its popularity with tourists.

2. Crete is **too big** to be able to do justice to it in a single holiday.

3. Cretan **cuisine** relies on fresh, seasonal vegetables and each season has new culinary delights.

4. **Walks and hikes** on Crete change with the seasons and each season is different.

5. More than 100 **gorges** are waiting to be explored by energetic adventurers.

6. The mountains are snow-covered in **winter**; it is worth the trip just to see that sight.

7. In Rethimnon they celebrate **carnival** in spectacular fashion.

8. The **museums** that have been closed for renovation will be reopened soon.

9. Every visitor to Crete helps the island to emerge from the **financial crisis**.

10. Most of the **hotels** offer good value for money.